GETTING
Value
FROM
PROFESSIONAL
ADVISERS

GETTING
Value
FROM
PROFESSIONAL
ADVISERS

HOW TO SAVE MONEY AND GET GOOD SERVICE

Catriona Standish

KOGAN
PAGE

To my family, for tolerating
professional uncertainties

First published in 1993

Apart from any fair dealing for the purposes of research or private
study, or criticism or review, as permitted under the Copyright,
Designs and Patents Act, 1988, this publication may only be
reproduced, stored or transmitted, in any form or by any means,
with the prior permission in writing of the publishers, or in the case
of reprographic reproduction in accordance with the terms of
licences issued by the Copyright Licensing Agency. Enquiries
concerning reproduction outside those terms should be sent to the
publishers at the undermentioned address:

Kogan Page Limited
120 Pentonville Road
London N1 9JN
© Catriona Standish, 1993

British Library Cataloguing in Publication Data

A CIP record for this book is available from the British Library.
ISBN 0 7494 1084 1

Typeset by Photoprint, Torquay, Devon
Printed and bound in Great Britain by Clay s Ltd, St Ives plc

Contents

1
Introduction

The importance of the professions and the professional classes can hardly be overrated, they form the head of the great English middle class, maintain its tone of independence, keep up to the mark its standard of morality and direct its intelligence.

(H Byerley Thomson, 1857)

This publication aims to save you money. Add up what you or your company spent on accountants, solicitors, surveyors, management consultants, architects, advertising and marketing expertise, patent agents and other business professionals last year. For most companies, this will not be an insignificant sum. Not everyone is fully aware of how professionals charge for their services. You may be embarrassed to query your professional's bill; perhaps he intimidates you with his degrees and plush office or international reputation.

Just remember this — you are the client. The professionals are there to serve you and they want your business. They depend on people like you for their livelihood. You are entitled to expect a decent service at an affordable price. If the sentiments expressed in the quotation above make you seethe with rage, read on. The professions have changed since 1857, as has the public's perception of them. Professionals are seen as a necessary evil by many users of their services — expensive and inaccessible. (Remember that Shakespeare in *Henry VI Pt. II* had Dick announcing, 'The first thing we do, let's kill all the lawyers'!)

Professionals have become increasingly commercialised and

now run their professional partnerships as businesses with marketing managers and in-house financial advisers to assist them. Certain professions are unlikely ever to come very high in the popularity stakes, but used properly your professional advisers can be a valuable business tool, improving your company's profitability and enabling it to exploit markets and develop business areas. At best, professional advisers will be confidential advisers, business facilitators and an independent shoulder to lean or cry upon.

This book seeks to improve the relationship between professional advisers and their clients. It will show you how to pick the best professionals for your needs and how to obtain good value from them. How can you keep their charges down, but ensure a good service? What about novel deals on billing? Many firms will listen responsively to requests for monthly billing, fixed price work, and more.

The early 1990s saw a major contraction of the demand for professional services. Large companies realised the power, as major purchasers of such services, that they can wield and used the opportunity to negotiate substantial reductions in professional fees. This publication should assist medium-sized and smaller companies and individuals in achieving the same types of savings and deals, in addition to improving their relationship with advisers. The boom bubble has burst. The days of massive fees and large annual increases in fee income are over for many professionals. The clients are the beneficiaries of the new realism, but only when armed with the knowledge of how to exploit their position. This book seeks to provide such knowledge.

CUTTING FEES

You can cut your professional advisers' fees if you act now.

1.   Prepare a list of all the professional advisers used by you or your firm. Complete the form in Appendix 1 for this purpose, if you wish. If you are responsible for a large group of companies, is there central control over which

professionals are chosen? Do you even know? Find out. It may save you money.

2. What sums have you paid over the last twelve months to each firm and on what basis? Again, use may be made of Appendix 1 for this purpose. On what basis were fees charged? List when bills were rendered and whether there has been any dispute over fees.

3. Are you aware of what your adviser did in incurring these fees? Were you happy with the service?

Even if you are entirely happy with the service given and the fees charged, this book should help you maintain the good working relationship which you have already developed with your professional adviser.

Reference should always be made to the appropriate professional body (see Appendix 2) for detail concerning their respective practices or professional conduct rules to which members are subject. There has been no attempt here to describe such professional rules in detail.

QUALITY OF ADVICE

Although cost is a major issue when instructing professional advisers, the quality of the advice is naturally vital. Most professionals are required to be members of what are, effectively, regulatory bodies and are required to meet defined standards, both as to professional competence and personal standards. Professions are made up of ordinary people, with the faults and differences which are evident in any job. Some will have greater competence than others; for instance, they may be especially clever or knowledgeable about their particular area. Most professions require that members sit what can be very difficult professional examinations, so, in general terms, there should be a basic level of competence common to all within a particular profession. However, not all professionals will have passed their examinations so well or even at the first attempt.

Going to a well recognised large professional practice can ensure that the individual professionals used have all attained high academic standards, because those firms will only recruit the cream of the profession: good 'A' levels, first or upper second class degrees, etc. There are, of course, high flyers in smaller practices, but it can be harder to spot them. In any event, professional examinations were, for many professionals, undertaken a significant number of years ago. Have they kept up to date with changes in their particular field? Does the profession require that members submit themselves to regular continuing education?

A number of professions stipulate that individuals practising in that profession regularly attend courses to keep up to date with recent developments. Learning that your professional adviser is speaking at a leading conference in the area on which you go to him for advice, or has written the principal textbook on the relevant area, certainly gives comfort to the client and is highly likely to indicate that the professional's knowledge is deep.

It may be that state-of-the-art, up-to-the-minute advice is really unnecessary for you. You may just want your factory premises conveyed or your books audited. Most professionals would pass the quality test in such cases. Chapter 3 looks at how to go about finding and instructing a professional adviser.

Ability to communicate

A clever professional does not necessarily make a good adviser. There is no disadvantage in brains and knowledge of the subject area; indeed, such knowledge is essential and what companies and individuals are paying for when instructing professional advisers. However, the professional must also have adequate personal skills, and be able to communicate well, whether orally or in writing, in order to pass on the information upon which advice has been sought in a way the client can understand.

Those wishing to instruct professionals should also ensure that their adviser is a person who relates well to other people. Is he excessively shy or domineering and bossy? Does he look at you when you speak to him and allow you to finish your sentences? Does he contribute fully to discussions or is he too reticent to offer significant views? Does he understand what you say to him and do you understand his answers? The question of how to maintain a good relationship with a professional adviser is considered in Chapter 5.

Offering advice

Equally important is the extent to which the adviser is able to apply his knowledge to your particular situation and think laterally as to how a problem can be accommodated or overcome. With age professionals improve their skills at thinking round problems and offering solutions. Some never learn and are content to spend the whole of their professional life churning out quotations from the law, or whatever the relevant field. Avoid such individuals at all costs; their advice may be useless to you.

Customer care

Professionals provide services to companies and individuals. They are one of the service industries and ought to adopt all the standards and concern for customer care which most large retail and other concerns have adopted in recent years. This is not always the case. You have a right to be treated with respect and deference. The client is always right. If the client is wrong, there are ways of telling him so without the discussion culminating in an argument.

Without the companies who instruct professional firms the firms themselves would not exist. Professionals are there to assist those in business.

THE BALANCE OF POWER

Some professionals are officious and arrogant. They believe too strongly that they are always in the right. They can be pompous and overbearing. Clients feel intimidated and do not dare to contribute to discussions, fearing they will look foolish if they let the professional know that they have not understood a word he was saying.

The antidote is that the client should always remember who is paying the professional fees. The client is buying a service in the same sense as any other service of the company is bought. Getting off on the right footing can ensure that the professional relationship enjoys the right balance or power. If you feel intimidated by the plush offices of your professional advisers invite them to meet at your offices, though bear in mind that you will have to pay for them to come to you, including paying for their travel expenses and time spent travelling. This might, however, be worth paying for to ensure that you feel comfortable. Your time is likely to be very valuable too and it can be sensible in forging a good relationship with professionals for them to have sight of the premises or factory from which you carry on business.

You may be intimidated by the vast number of people whom the professional brings along to meetings, which obviously increases the cost. As discussed in Chapter 4, consider informing the professional that you are not prepared to pay for non-essential participants at a meeting.

When meeting a professional adviser or speaking over the telephone for the first time, ensure that you establish the upper hand. If the professional begins talking in jargon or you cannot understand him for any reason, say so: firmly, but politely, explain that you require clear and simple advice and that you will always let him know when he can improve in this area.

Be authoritative even if you do not feel like it. Develop a firm handshake. Above all, stand up to these people. The fact that they have passed examinations and are allowed to apply a grandiose title to their activities does not make them any better than you are. You, and others like you, are the source of the professionals' supposed power and actual wealth. Without those upon whom such service industries depend, there would be no service provision at all. Treat professionals as equals, politely and 'professionally', and expect this treatment to be reciprocated. If it is not, go elsewhere.

In no circumstances be daunted by supposed professional mystique. It should not exist. The professionals have services which you need. There are many professionals, all competing with each other to offer you services. They want you to give them your business. Always bear this essential factor in mind in your relationships with professionals: they are there to serve.

The good professionals

This book dwells on the negative side of professional relationships, because that is where help and advice are needed. It necessarily highlights areas where things can go wrong, such as arguments over bills, unintelligible advice, arrogant professionals. In so doing it inevitably conveys the impression that professional relationships are difficult and unpleasant. In fact, in many cases professionals and their clients enjoy a happy and harmonious relationship to the mutual benefit of both parties. Many professionals thrive in business because they understand the needs of the client and have a good rapport with other people. They talk about problems before those problems grow into intractable disputes and always discuss bills and billing arrangements in advance so that the matter of fees is settled to the satisfaction of both parties.

If you enjoy such a good relationship with your professional advisers, this book may still be of assistance. It is not every adviser who is good in all areas. There will almost always be at least one area where the relationship can be improved. Bills can always be reduced, or different billing arrangements negotiated, as discussed in Chapter 4.

Do not assume that all professionals are difficult people with whom to establish a harmonious relationship will be hard. False preconceptions may lead to problems for both parties. Expecting a professional adviser to overcharge or offer impractical help and adopting an attitude of resigned expectation that this will be the case can lead to the very problem which is sought to be overcome.

Expect the best and negotiate upwards from the worst if necessary.

The assumption that you are a small and insignificant client of the professional adviser and cannot therefore expect a reply to correspondence for at least a fortnight is not the way towards a happy relationship with such advisers. Call the adviser if no response materialises, at least by way of acknowledgement to your letter, and make it clear when you expect to hear from him. Be conscious of your own importance and make that positive attitude come over in how you speak and write to the professional adviser. Develop your self-confidence as much in your relationship with the adviser as you ought in dealings with the clients of your company or enterprise.

By dwelling on problems with professionals, this book does give a warped picture of such relationships. However, there is no difficulty in being pleasantly surprised when you deal with professionals. Being forewarned of potential problem areas should ensure that you are able to obtain better value from all professional advisers, whatever their merits and whatever areas of weakness they suffer from in their professional dealings.

The inadequate client

It ought not to be heresy in a book of this sort to suggest that clients, too, are capable of improvement. The emphasis in this book is on how to obtain better value from advisers; this is a two-way process. There is much that a client can do to obtain better value for money:

1. Give clear and full written instructions to the adviser.
2. Tell him your commercial aims. Do not leave him to guess.
3. Be honest. There is no merit in lying, or massaging the facts, to those who are on your side and whom you are paying to advise you.
4. Instruct him positively and wholeheartedly. Show enthusiasm in your dealings with the professional adviser.
5. Respond to requests for information punctually and efficiently. Send all relevant papers and not just those upon which you can most easily lay your hands.
6. Raise problems early.
7. Pay professional bills on time.

The example below illustrates the operation of professional relationships at their best and worst.

John Smith telephones his solicitor, Septimus Dollar, when he reads an article in a trade magazine about a new EC health and safety measure which appears likely to have a significant impact on his business. Septimus knows nothing about this area of law. Very competent at advising on the basics of corporate law, the solicitor does not follow EC law developments and knows very little about UK health and safety legislation. John Smith says very little to Septimus. He does not explain how he sees the potential impact of the measure on his busines or which of his products are in the relevant area. He just says that he wants some advice on what this measure is likely to mean for him. He gives no timescale for when he requires the advice, although he has an important board meeting in two days' time at which he is concerned that the issue may be raised, nor does he state whether he wants advice in writing or over the telephone.

Septimus has had a quiet week, mostly spent undertaking various nebulous marketing matters. Here is something to get his teeth into. He begins by involving his trainee and having him find all old, new and proposed legislation in the field. He sits down with all the relevant measures and produces a detailed memorandum on the measure concerned. This runs to 20 pages and considers the impact of the proposed new law over all business areas.

In fact, John Smith's employer is involved in only one of a considerable number of fields which are dealt with by the measure. Septimus did not think of telephoning John Smith to ask him for more information about what is required before proceeding.

John Smith telephones Septimus on the eve of the board meeting, asking if he yet has any advice for him. Septimus' memorandum is not ready. 'So what's it all about then, this new law?', John Smith asks.

Septimus, who has read the proposal carefully, finds it difficult to express himself over the telephone and has not really thought through the implications of the measure. He begins a long and involved explanation for the benefit of the client, which leaves the client no wiser. The client is promised the memorandum as soon as possible and when he is asked about the measure at the board meeting, is only able to say that he is seeking legal advice.

When he receives the memorandum the following week, it is so long he puts it away and never looks at it again. Two months later John Smith receives a bill for over £1000, representing the time, charged at £150 per hour, which Septimus has spent acquainting himself with this area. The client refuses to pay and a major argument ensues.

What should have happened is that Septimus, on being asked for advice, tells the client that this is not an area with which he is familiar and suggests that the client telephone the Health and Safety Executive, which could have informed the client of the practical implications of this measure for his area of business free of charge. Septimus could, alternatively, have obtained more specific instructions from the client about exactly what was required and within what timescale.

John Smith should have faxed through the article he had read advising him of the measure, from which it was obvious what the only relevant point for his business was. John Smith should have asked for an estimate of the charges and requested a telephone call on the day before the conference with a short, one-page letter summarising the change as it affects the relevant area.

Communication is at the heart of successful professional relationships. The above example illustrates how important it is for both parties to communicate effectively with each other.

CHECKLIST

- Find out what professional fees you have paid over the last 12 months

- Assess your degree of satisfaction with the services performed, not only in terms of value for money, but also quality of advice and ability to communicate

- Remember that you are the customer. Do not be intimidated by a professional adviser. Be authoritative and assertive

- Be a good client — give clear instructions, tell your adviser your aims, be honest, show enthusiasm, respond quickly to requests for information, raise problems early and pay bills on time

- Good communication is at the heart of successful professional relationships

2

The professionals

The chief difference between a profession and a trade or business is, that in the case of a profession its members sacrifice a certain amount of individual liberty in order to ensure certain professional objects. In a trade or business the conduct of each individual is avowedly regulated simply by the general rules of honesty and regard to his own interest.

(A V Dicey, 1867)

Although there is considerable dispute about which people should be called 'professionals', and most people with skills like to believe that they fall within this term, in practice the term, as used in this book, has been taken to include the following:

- accountants;
- solicitors and barristers;
- management consultants;
- marketing and advertising advisers;
- surveyors;
- architects;
- patent and trademark agents;
- merchant bankers.

These are all people who provide services rather than goods, and who offer business advice to companies and individuals. However, many of the methods set out in this book concerning how to choose and appoint professionals would apply equally to any other appointment. People who might also be termed professionals include actuaries, loss adjusters and insurance agents and brokers and, no doubt, many others. What professionals often have in common is a certain mystique, not always earned, over the work they undertake.

Professionals generally undertake skilled and specialised work, most of which is mental rather than manual. They undergo a period of training before qualification. They are required to follow certain moral principles with high standards of service and special obligations to their clients, such as obligations of confidentiality. Generally, professionals are members of a self-regulating professional body and are regarded as enjoying high status within the community.

The term 'profession' used to be confined to the Church, medicine and the law; of these three, only the last is considered in this book. The categories of professionals change over time and today many are regarded as professionals who, a century ago, would not have enjoyed such status.

Many professionals are still held in awe by clients and this does not always lead to a useful and profitable relationship between professional and client. There is frequently a tacit assumption that the client cannot understand the work which the professional does. 'Leave it all to me, old chap. I know what I'm doing,' some professionals say. Knowledge of what the professional does is very useful in breaking down the barriers which the mystique erects. The professional may possibly have more examination passes than the client or more knowledge in a particular area, but that is why the professional has been consulted in the first place. This does not mean that the client cannot understand the basics of the work which is to be done.

Knowledge gives greater control to the client over the professional and can assist the professional, who then does not need to explain everything to the client.

Above all, the client should ask questions, not just of the professional, but also of friends, acquaintances and contacts who work in the same profession. If the client has the time and is sufficiently interested, books may be available on the relevant subject-matter on which the professional has been consulted. There is certainly no obligation on the part of the client to delve into much detail if he does not want to do so. He may be placing matters in the hands of the professional in order to take the burden of dealing with this area off his own shoulders, but in terms of getting better value from the professionals, knowing what they are doing assists.

If a professional responds to a question concerning the work to be done by baffling you with science or jargon, demand a simple explanation. The best experts are those who can explain their subject-matter as if to a child in a clear fashion. If the explanation seems muddled, it may be that the professional is muddled.

Effective communication is considered in detail in Chapter 5, but always ensure that both client and professional are speaking the same language. The professional may have a fundamental lack of understanding of the facts upon which his advice is to be based. Having the professional recite the facts he has been told, and apply the advice to them, will enable the client to ascertain whether he has passed on clearly and accurately the nature of the problem which concerned him.

This chapter looks at a number of different professionals and their role, background and training. It is not comprehensive because there are in practice so many different situations where advice is needed from various forms of professionals. However it does cover the essential role of most of the main professionals used by businesses and individuals today.

ACCOUNTANTS

Accountants are for many companies the most frequently used professionals. Indeed, limited companies are obliged by law to engage accountants to act as auditors, although there are proposals at the time of writing to remove this requirement for smaller companies. As the law presently stands, there is no choice. Accounts must be audited externally each year. This can be a good discipline for all companies, small and large.

Accountants offer a broad range of services to companies, ranging from auditing to the provision of financial and other management consultants, tax advice and insolvency services. Accountants will be members of one of the five main accountancy bodies:

1. The Institute of Chartered Accountants of England and Wales (ICAEW).
2. The Institute of Chartered Accountants of Scotland (ICAS).
3. The Chartered Institute of Certified Accountants (CICA).
4. The Chartered Institute of Management Accountants (CIMA).
5. The Chartered Institute of Public Finance and Accountancy (CIPFA).

The Institute of Chartered Accountants of England and Wales (ICAEW) is one of the largest professional bodies in the world with over 100,000 members. About half the members work in accountancy practices and half in industry and commerce or the public sector. Their training takes up to four years before they may use the letters 'ACA' (or 'FCA' after a further ten years denoting fellowship of the Institute). The equivalent body in Scotland is the Institute of Chartered Accountants of Scotland (ICAS).

The Chartered Institute of Certified Accountants (CICA) has a similar system, with members using the designation 'ACCA'. Members of the ICAEW, ICAS and ACCA may legally audit company accounts. Members of other accountancy bodies have no legal right to do so and should not be engaged for that purpose. The Chartered Institute of Management Accountants has over 33,000 members throughout the world. Members of the Chartered Institute of Public Finance and Accountancy are usually employed in the public sector and are therefore unlikely to be engaged by those wishing to consult an accountant.

Training and professional structure

Accountants' training consists of a first degree, not necessarily in accountancy, followed by a period of training at an accountancy practice, during which time professional examinations are sat. Accountancy practices are run as partnerships of self-employed individuals, who employ other accountants and trainees to assist them. Your work may be undertaken by either a partner or an employed qualified accountant or an accountant still undergoing training who has not yet passed all the relevant professional examinations.

There is no simple answer to the question of which type of practitioner within an accountancy practice you should be using. The less qualified an individual, the less it will generally cost you, though highly competent partners may be able to undertake your work quickly and more efficiently than those still learning on the job. It is a question to be determined not only in relation to each new client of a practice, but also for each piece of work from that client. Where a more junior member of staff undertakes your work, he or she is likely to be supervised by a partner of the firm. You can express an opinion on the type of person whom you wish to carry out your work, though by and large the practice will allocate staff as it sees fit.

Companies should keep under review the firms which they use for external auditing purposes and ensure that value for money continues to be obtained year by year. Sometimes an inertia factor operates here; it may seem simpler to continue to use the same practice for years. However, practices do change. Your company may expand and require the services of a major firm of accountants for image purposes or conversely the professional practice may grow or merge to the extent that your small company becomes a relatively unimportant client; moving to a practice where you are seen as a major client may ensure better service.

Keep a constant annual check on the fee charged. If you are presented with a much larger bill than in previous years, ask for the reasons and determine whether or not those reasons appear sufficiently plausible, or whether for the following year another practice should be used.

Accountants, of course, do much more than auditing. Advice can be sought for a large variety of business reasons. Insolvency advice may be needed or a company may want advice on how to structure, from a tax point of view, the operation of a new business abroad. Should a new subsidiary company be set up in the country concerned or would the company pay less tax through operating directly in such country or should it set up an intermediate holding company in a favourable tax haven?

Not all accountants will have the expert knowledge to advise on these areas. The difficulty for the client lies in knowing that there are questions of this type to be asked if the accountant concerned is unaware of the options available. Ensuring a basic knowledge within your company of the types of problems upon which advice is needed can ensure that the right questions are, in fact, asked, rather than completely overlooked. The best professionals will either advise on points of this sort or at least be aware that specialist advice is needed and refer the client to another practice from whom such advice can be obtained.

Which professionals to use

Staying with the tax example, the question of which professionals to use arises: not only is there the issue of choosing between different firms of accountants, but also between types of professionals. Many major solicitors' practices now advise on tax law and if a company is, as in the example here, considering setting up in business abroad, then it will probably be using the service of a solicitor already, who may be qualified to give the advice required.

It is obvious, but worth repeating that, as a general rule, the more professionals involved, the larger the bill. This applies not only within individual professional firms, but also across different disciplines. Many professional bodies forbid professionals from entering into partnership with different types of professional, though increasingly there are moves to relax the rules of the bodies concerned. So do not blame your professional because he does not have partners who are expert in a number of different disciplines, though many firms do employ experts from other professions.

Recommendations by accountants of other professionals

Accountants are usually the first port of call for many businesses who need professional advice over a wide range of issues. They can therefore wield considerable power. If your accountants recommend another professional firm, there is no obligation for you to accept that recommendation. There may be some system of mutual referrals in operation, which may benefit the professionals, but not necessarily you. As with any other area of business, shopping around often achieves the best value for money. Simply proceeding with the recommendation of your accountants or other professionals may not be in your best interests.

In each case, ask the accountants why they are suggesting a particular firm, whether they have used them in the past and whether you can speak to other clients of the accountants who have been referred to the same firm. Obtaining details of a number of past users will enable you to sound out over the telephone those names put forward. However, bear in mind that the accountants are unlikely to put forward names of clients who have not been happy with a recommendation.

Do not discount recommendations entirely. As will be seen in Chapter 3, recommendation is often the best method of choosing a professional and if an accountancy practice regularly recommends work to another type of professional practice, that other practice is likely to feel under an obligation to offer a good service, if it wants the recommendations to continue to flow. Simply accept the recommendation with some measure of caution and see other practices too, if there is time, to enable a clear choice to be made.

Accountants will provide management consultancy services and advice over a wide range of business areas. Although there can be cost savings in one-stop shopping, be cautious about practices which appear to offer too much. For example, an accountancy firm offering information technology consulting and advice on computer systems may employ experts from the computer industry, who possess great competence. Those individuals, however, are unlikely to have had the legal training necessary to give advice concerning the drafting of agreements in this area.

Accountants will be able to offer more than a 'reacting' type of service, responding to questions put by the client. They should be business advisers, able to give general, impartial advice about how the business is doing in terms of profitability, structure and product ranges, and how it should expand or otherwise in the future.

SOLICITORS

There is no requirement for any company to use solicitors, although in many cases it would be foolish not to do so.

Individuals have rights to represent themselves in court and take proceedings, as well as to draw up commercial agreements and undertake conveyancing work. However, unless there is a solicitor employed by the company who is familiar with the relevant area, it is unwise to seek to manage without legal advice.

A solicitor may be required to set up a new company and advise on whether the business should be run as a company, partnership or some other structure. Although companies can be purchased 'off-the-peg' from company agents, it may be more straightforward to have a solicitor responsible for ensuring that all legal requirements are met. Many new companies seek to begin in business using only accountants. Solicitors may not be used until something goes wrong.

This is not always the best way to act. It may be possible to avert the matter which 'goes wrong' by obtaining legal advice in the first place. The company may, for example, set up in business under a chosen business name, have stationery printed and a shop facia prepared, only to discover that another company operates under the same name. Legal action may then be initiated against such a company; how much better if that advice had been obtained beforehand.

Initial advice is recommended, but this need not mean huge bills for a new company which is strapped for cash. Pick a relatively inexpensive solicitor at the outset and explain the financial position of the company. Dangle before him the carrot that the company is likely to become sizeable and profitable soon and it is worth his while offering a very cost-effective service now, as there will be much more profitable work later. Then obtain only basic essential advice. The advantage of finding a practice early means that the effort of choosing the best practice for the particular company will have been undertaken in comparative leisure, using the guidelines in Chapter 3, and a better choice will probably have been made than by having to ring round frantically when the first writ against the company arrives. There would not be much chance for careful choice then, when legal proceedings have strict time limits.

Once a company is operating, a solicitor might be used for a variety of tasks, not all of which do require expert help. It really depends on the company concerned, and the individuals within it, as to the extent to which the solicitor will be used. Some business owners and managers are more than happy to play a quasi-legal role and call in the solicitor when needed. Others want the assurance and time-saving of placing all such matters firmly in the solicitor's hands.

Examples of work which is undertaken within companies without necessarily using a solicitor include:

- drawing up conditions of employment;
- drafting agreements such as distribution agreements, patent licensing agreements and terms and conditions of sale;
- sacking staff.

Many companies frequently do undertake such activities without advice. There are inherent dangers in this approach, though it is certainly cheaper unless things go wrong. Is there a compromise? Using a competitor's terms and conditions or commercially available standard guidelines can give some reassurance that the documents used probably cover all the points which ought to be addressed in the relevant agreement.

Use all precedents (ie commercially produced pro forma standard agreements) with caution. They will have been drawn up with particular situations in mind, which may not mirror exactly the situation with which you are concerned. If undertaking the drafting of commercial agreements on your own, remember the following:

- Say what you mean.
- Make sure, if you change a clause in a precedent, that all the 'knock-on' effects throughout the document are appreciated.
- Do not be lazy about such matters as consistent clause numbers, the correct spelling of the parties, the cross-referencing of provisions.
- Make sure that all parties sign the document and that it is then dated. The full legal names of all parties should appear.

Economic circumstance may make this type of approach necessary, but it is often preferable to consult a solicitor. To save money in that process, send your draft with all the relevant provisions early on in a transaction to your solicitor for a quick 'vet', rather than leaving the professional to produce all the text himself.

Solicitors will usually be needed when you want to sue another company or are being sued. The threat of legal proceedings can be frightening; using a solicitor should provide reassurance and ensure that your rights are protected in the best way possible. The drafting of a defence, or preparing a statement of claim on a writ, really requires expert help. Although it is possible to draw up some forms of commercial agreement without legal assistance, litigation should not usually be undertaken without a solicitor's help.

If a company must represent itself, then free legal advice may be available from organisations, such as the Citizens' Advice Bureau or Law Centres, though they may be unable to provide assistance to companies involved in complex commercial litigation. Companies suffering from bad debts may go to a debt collection agency or factor their debts instead of suing. Those wanting conveyancing undertaken can instruct licensed conveyancers, though this option may not necessarily be any cheaper than using a solicitor.

For individuals, free legal advice may be available to the very poor through the legal aid scheme. Books contain advice for those who wish to draw up a will, get divorced or recover a debt in the small claims court — viable alternatives for those who cannot afford, or choose not to use, solicitors.

Solicitors will be involved in a large number of other areas upon which advice may be sought. Companies taking on the substantial financial commitment of the purchase or lease of a property would be very unwise not to engage a solicitor. Similarly, those entering into joint venture, partnership or merger agreements, or those buying or selling a business, should be legally advised. Although there are methods of saving money on fees, discussed later in this book, a solicitor still needs to be instructed.

Sacking an employee is generally better done after a discussion with a solicitor, particularly if there are likely to be unfair dismissal or redundancy claims. Ensuring that employment law is complied with beforehand is preferable to making the dismissal and then being faced with proceedings before an industrial tribunal — a situation which could have been avoided, had the matter been properly handled originally.

In summary, the best advice is to consult early and minimally if cost is an inhibiting factor. For litigation, buying and selling, and hiring and firing, advice should be sought. There is a vast range of other areas in which, for particular companies, legal advice should be obtained. Examples are where a company sets up in business with employees from another company and trade secrets may be being used, or where a company wishes to set up a trust or pension fund or enter the complex EC market.

It is essential to develop the commercial know-how to be able to discern where there may be a legal problem. It is not necessary to know what the exact problem is or how to solve it; that is the professional's job, but knowing that the problem is there should ensure that the right steps are taken in time. Being blind to the problem will mean that advice is not sought when needed.

Training and professional structure

Solicitors usually hold a university degree, often in law, and then proceed to take the Law Society's professional examinations, followed by two years as a trainee with a firm, previously known as serving articles of clerkship. During that training period trainees may be allocated to work for you. It is important that those engaging solicitors are aware of the status of members of the firm with whom they are likely to deal. Solicitors are regulated by the Law Society (details in Appendix 2).

Work undertaken for clients by trainees is charged to the client, but at a cheaper rate than that done by qualified practitioners. The use of a trainee may be justifiable for mundane jobs such as checking documents, arranging enclosures, assisting in drafting letters and agreements, but beware of the problems caused by double-manning: the partner bringing his trainee along should be able to justify that individual's presence. Such justification might rightly be that the trainee or other junior assistant will, after the meeting, be required to prepare a note of the meeting or prepare some documents. However, if the trainee is present at a meeting without justification, then it is your right to query this and suggest that because you appreciate the importance of training new professionals and what can be learnt through attendance at meetings, the trainee may remain, but on a non-chargeable basis.

Once qualified, a solicitor joins a practice as an employee and is usually known as an assistant solicitor. Solicitors do not gain additional letters after their name on becoming qualified; they simply have the right to call themselves 'solicitor of the Supreme Court' or 'solicitor'. Thereafter they may be offered a partnership in the practice, sometimes with rather grandiose-sounding, but practically unimportant, staging-posts on the way of 'associate' or 'senior solicitor'. Partners will either all be equity partners, sharing in the profits and losses of the practice; or else junior partners may be admitted as salaried partners without, at first, a profit share.

Many solicitors' practices employ legal executives to assist them. Such individuals will have taken the examinations of the Institute of Legal Executives and will be either a student or, after taking Parts 1 and 2 examinations, a member who, after two years in practice, will become a Fellow of the Institute. Fellows are entitled to use the initials FInstLEX. Legal executives cannot become partners in solicitors' practices and do not generally have university degrees; and it is fair to say that their professional examinations are not as difficult as those required to become a solicitor. They do have a useful role to play in assisting the work of solicitors and in practice, after several years' experience, examinations become less an indication of competence than do experience and the ability to undertake legal work competently.

It is useful to have some idea of the status of the individuals within the solicitors' practice with whom you deal. If you are not told, ask. Ask the individual concerned how long he or she has been with the firm and how long he or she has been qualified and, if you are unhappy about the level of experience which that person appears to have, then address the issue tactfully with the partner in charge. Alternatively, you may feel that a partner with high charging rates has been allocated to your case, where really it is a simple case which could just as easily and more cheaply be dealt with by someone more junior. If so, say so.

Legal expenses insurance

All companies should consider taking out legal expenses insurance. Although when a legal case is successfully undertaken a proportion of your legal costs will be recoverable from the other side, this will not cover all costs; also, you may not win. Your solicitor will still have to be paid. A number of insurance companies offer insurance cover against legal expenses. If such a policy is bought, then its terms should be examined carefully in advance.

Both personal and commercial cover is available up to various financial limits and for different areas. Some companies will only provide cover where there are reasonable prospects of success in relation to a particular legal suit. Companies offering commercial cover include Abbey Life Protection, DAS Legal Expenses Insurance, Legal Protection Group and Hambro LP.

Some policies are not very comprehensive and, indeed, may not cover the legal areas in which the purchaser of the policy expects most to make claims, so study the policy carefully and do not rely on the statements of over-enthusiastic salesmen. Keep the price of the policy under review.

Finally, solicitors may be a form of insurance policy too. If they give negligent advice which causes you loss, there may be a cause of action against them. They will have insurance cover against such actions. Suing professional advisers is covered in Chapter 7.

BARRISTERS

Barristers have rights of audience before all courts, a general right presently denied to solicitors, who only enjoy limited rights of audience. In undertaking litigation, therefore, a barrister will be retained by your solicitor on your behalf. You have a right to choose who is instructed and there is no obligation to accept the recommendation of the solicitor (although there may be very good reasons why a particular barrister has been chosen, for example, because he or she is an expert in the particular area to which your case relates).

The reputation and ability of the barrister, and his or her familiarity with the area of law concerned, should be the overriding factors determining who is selected. However, sight should not be lost of cost; barristers' clerks will inform your solicitor of the barrister's charges and this enables comparisons to be made. It will also be necessary to determine whether you need to engage a 'junior' barrister or a Queen's Counsel (QC) and a junior together. Much will depend on the nature of the case and how much money is at stake.

Beware of solicitors' practices which seem to be sending all difficult points on areas of law where you need advice to 'counsel' (the term used for barristers). This may be because the solicitor whom you have chosen does not know enough about the relevant area of law. It may be cheaper to choose a solicitor's practice which has experience in the legal area concerned. Although in the past many general solicitors' practices would not be expected to be knowledgeable in all areas, these days most competent commercial practices should be able to offer in-house experts over a full range of the law. They will not consult counsel for an 'opinion' unless there is a very difficult question of law on which the client needs a second opinion. Counsel's opinions do have their place and can be very useful in persuading a company which is threatening to sue you, or is reluctant to part with money owed or perform the terms of a contract, that the law is on your side.

Counsel has a very useful role to play when litigation is in prospect, but, for general commercial law advice, that of an expert solicitor is likely to be cheaper and as good. Generally, your solicitor will be the 'interface' between the barrister and you, but some in-house legal departments of large companies frequently instruct counsel themselves.

Training and professional structure

Barristers, like solicitors, usually have a law degree, but have followed that up with their Bar Finals course rather than the solicitors' professional examination. Barristers then spend time as a pupil barrister, undertaking what is known as pupillage, before seeking a tenancy (ie a place) in chambers (set of rooms, usually in Inns of Court). Barristers are regulated by the General Council of the Bar (details in Appendix 2).

Barristers practise together in chambers, but each barrister is self-employed, rather than operating in the form of partnerships like solicitors. Chambers employ a clerk, a very powerful and often lucrative position. The clerk arranges which barrister is consulted and agrees the fees, retaining a percentage as his remuneration.

MANAGEMENT CONSULTANTS

Management consultants are frequently accountants, engineers or ex-business managers, who are giving the benefit of their expertise to other businesses for a fee. Their role varies widely depending on what the business requires. For example, a management consultant might be hired to assist in ironing out production problems experienced by a company, or to help it with choosing and putting in place an expensive new computer system.

As with all professionals, it is important to ensure that each party knows the respective roles and expectations of the other. The management consultants who will be working at the offices of the hiring company should be people, particularly in small companies, with whom those involved feel they can happily work. Always ask to see the curricula vitae of individual management consultants who are put forward to assist your company.

Make enquiries about the general previous experience of the consultants concerned. Ask for a list of clients, particularly those for whom they have undertaken similar assignments, and select a few to contact for references. Many consultancies have sprung up, not only to meet demand, but also through force of economic circumstances. It can be an easy answer for those who have been made redundant, with many years of valuable business experience behind them, to set themselves up as management consultants. In many cases they do have valuable skills which can be passed on, but not everyone has the ability to impart ideas clearly rather than just be competent at carrying out a practising management role. As with other professionals, obtaining a recommendation should ensure that the worst practices are avoided.

The types of management consultants most commonly required work in the following areas.

Business strategy

This is giving advice on what direction a company should take for its future development, and whether new products, different prices or markets or methods of distribution could profitably be developed. Strategy consultants should have relevant qualifications, such as an accountancy or marketing qualification or an MBA, and experience in the field.

Organisation design and development

This means advising on internal structures and communication problems. Such consultants will aim to improve employee morale and ensure that all employees are aware of the direction of the company and its ultimate strategy. Consultants in this area ought to have a relevant qualification, perhaps a first degree in psychology followed by a post-graduate qualification in the relevant area.

Financial management

Such consultants will cover a broad area, including taxation, mergers and acquisitions, investment strategy, credit and debt management. Consultants in this field would be expected to have an accountancy qualification (see page 23).

Quality management and manufacturing systems

These consultants advise on the systems necessary to ensure that customers receive the quality of product or service they require and advise on manufacturing and productivity. Check to see that the consultant has engineering experience.

> **Beware of professionals who seek to market their services to you or your company on the back of recent legislation.**

Examples include companies suggesting that all electrical appliances must be checked annually and they are the people to do so, when the law, as it presently stands, does not stipulate a period; or some of the cowboy operators who have set themselves up to assist companies to comply with BS Quality Standard 5750, a standard often required in contracts available for tender and for which many companies have been clamouring.

With BS5750, companies have spent thousands of pounds in order to obtain accreditation. There is no qualification needed to award the certificate which shows that a company's internal procedures are properly organised. There is no requirement to register with the National Accreditation Council of Certification Bodies, although some companies have obtained such accreditation. The costs of meeting the standard are high. Several thousand pounds will generally be spent in obtaining the certificate in the first place, and subsequent annual charges to ensure continued compliance may amount to £2000.

Computer and information technology

These consultants, many with a computer background, will advise on the computer or IT requirements of a company, including choice of systems, and also provide advice on how information can best be transferred within a company.

Project management

This type of consultant will be used for specific projects, such as a construction project or an ongoing project. Their role will be to pull everything together, taking over the day-to-day running of a particular project, liaising with the other individuals and professionals used to complete the project. Such consultants should be chosen carefully to ensure that they have the right skills to run a project. They may be members of the Chartered Institute of Building or of the Institute of Mechanical Engineers, or similar organisations.

Personnel management

Recruitment of staff, appraisal of performance, health and safety, dismissal and personnel records are all the territory of the personnel management consultant. Recruitment consultancies will be one discrete form of personnel management consultancy. Others may be brought in to provide training for employees or to design an employee appraisal system. Individuals may be members of the Institute of Personnel Management.

Marketing

Marketing consultants will assist companies in all aspects of marketing their products, looking at the market in which a company operates and its competitors and customers, or undertaking a marketing audit. Some consultants will be experts in direct marketing and sales promotions and others in the field of market research and public relations, or they may be an advertising agency. Consultants may possess a marketing diploma, such as that offered by the Chartered Institute of Marketing. Marketing and advertising advisers are discussed as a separate category below.

Design

These consultants will advise on both the aesthetic design of products which a company offers and also the impact such design has on factors like profitability. Industrial designers need to be familiar not only with UK technical standards for products, but also with EC and international standards.

Property management

Individuals involved in this field will often be surveyors, discussed below.

Transport management

These consultants will advise on any aspect of transport. The Post Office and British Rail offer transport advice and many consultants in this field will advise on the maintenance and management of a company car or van fleet, and assist with the buying of vehicles or their leasing.

Whether it is necessary to hire management consultants at all, and if so of which type, will depend on the needs of the company concerned. There may be no need ever to hire them and many companies are very efficiently run without having to call in such professional outside help. However, beware of being blinkered and assume that because the business is ticking over, there is therefore no need for help. It can be extremely useful to have an outside third party cast a fresh, independent eye over a business. Consultants may be able to isolate areas where you were not aware that improvement could be made and ensure that substantial cost savings result. Some professionals in this area may be prepared to negotiate some form of fee structure based on results, although this is not the norm and, indeed, is forbidden by the Management Consultancies Association. (As management consultants are involved in such a wide variety of fields it is not possible to list all the bodies of which they might have membership.)

Simply ensure that you are sceptical when a potential consultant mentions a body of which he or she has membership. It may not be a particularly large or well regarded organisation. Unlike some professions which are tightly regulated, such as accountants by the Institute of Chartered Accountants and solicitors by the Law Society, some organisations in this field may not be engaged in any effective regulation of their members at all.

MARKETING AND ADVERTISING ADVISERS

There are a large number of companies specialising in marketing and advertising or other public relations functions. Their role will vary depending on the needs of the client. Some companies may simply want advice on the design of their new stationery or business publications in order to achieve the best visual image. Others will want an advertising agency to take total charge of their marketing and advertising needs, expecting the agency to produce a range of potential advertisements for TV, posters, magazine advertisements and so forth. The engaging company will, of course, choose which of a number of alternative campaigns is ultimately adopted, but the agency has a very important role in advising on the strategy best suited to achieve the marketing aims of the company concerned. Public relations agencies will have details of publications in which advertisements can be placed and be able to arrange to issue press releases.

Are such agencies needed at all? Some companies have chosen not to spend on advertising at all or simply place their own advertisements in publications of which they are aware. Most large companies do employ agents in this field and many are very happy with the services provided to them. However, free publicity can be obtained through editorial coverage such as newspaper articles. Maintaining good relationships with journalists and simply providing good products which customers then recommend to others can result in business growth without involving expensive advertising consultants.

This area can be subdivided into public relations people, who simply assist in increasing goodwill and exposure of a company in the press and through other media, and advertising agencies, who run whole advertising campaigns for clients. Some professionals in this field will specialise in marketing, analysing your customers, and advise on your marketing strategy. Other subdivisions in this field include sales promotion and market research advisers.

One of the difficulties in determining what professional help is needed in this field is that advertising and marketing do not, as a general rule, produce an immediate pay-back. Although an advertisement by way of a mail order, 'money off the page' advertisement may result in a fixed number of orders placed, in most cases the public exposure resulting from the article, advertisement, flysheet or poster simply heightens public awareness of the actual product. It is possible to discover how frequently the agency has managed to have the company's name mentioned in the press and to set targets or goals in this field to assess performance.

> **It is important that money is not simply handed over to such professionals without there being any mechanism to check effectiveness of advertising campaigns run.**

These professionals will not just run advertising campaigns; they will offer advice over a broad range of marketing areas. Should the company run direct advertisements at all? Should it market itself at trade fairs? Through which publications will it get the best exposure? The professional will advise on how best to set up and effect interviews with the press and will send out appropriate press releases when there are new developments within the business, whether relating to new personnel or new products being launched.

When choosing whether or not to employ such professionals it can be useful to examine the activities of your competitors. Whom do they use and to what effect? Has their public profile been raised since they used a particular firm? Have you lost market share through an agressive new competitor employing certain public relations people or advertising agents?

For smaller companies, or those of any size who have not employed any outside assistance in this field before, the question will arise as to whether it is necessary. There are likely to be employees of your company who already undertake a considerable amount of marketing. Yours may be a business area where showing at trade fairs, together with a few strategically placed advertisements in the main trade publications, may achieve all the public exposure you need. However, it may be wise to consider employing, either on an occasional basis or on a small retainer, some PR agents who will assist you, through their contacts with journalists, in achieving exposure in the press and will advise you on making your publications look modern and in a consistent house style. The amount of money which a company has available to spend will largely determine what level of service is obtained from the agency.

Always enquire about the experience of the company which is proposed for use.

Find out who else uses them. Many companies would not consider using an agency which their closest competitor uses, but some agencies have particular experience in certain business sectors. Picking an agency with previous experience of a sector can ensure that they already have useful contacts in that field. Setting an advertising budget for the year will be part of the business plans of most companies. Ensuring that a fee is agreed with the advertising agency can be part of that process.

What size of agency to use is another issue. Small agencies are more likely to see your business as important to them, but they may be unable to handle a major advertising campaign. The larger agencies tend to charge more, but will have significant expertise. Developing a good relationship with one individual or several in a large agency, and ensuring that your company always uses these people with whom you are familiar, assists in ensuring that a smaller company using a large agency does not become lost and get passed from one person to another.

As already mentioned, when considering the role of marketing consultants, individuals in this field may have a diploma from the Institute of Marketing or qualifications in the design field, for example in graphics. There are a number of bodies of which such individuals might have membership, including the Advertising Association, the Direct Marketing Association, the Chartered Institute of Marketing and the Public Relations Consultants Association. It is always worth enquiring further about associations of which consultants proudly claim membership.

SURVEYORS

Most people who have purchased a house have experience of surveyors and are aware of their role in that kind of transaction in undertaking a survey of property. Surveyors, of course, have a much wider role than that and will be involved in all stages of the building of commercial premises. There are approximately 64,000 members of the Royal Institution of Chartered Surveyors, who are involved in private practice, companies and local government.

Those engaging surveyors will choose them from private practice. As with solicitors and accountants, practices will comprise employees and partners. Surveyors are regulated by the Royal Institution of Chartered Surveyors (details in Appendix 2). Some surveyors will be employed as consultants undertaking repairs to buildings and arranging and effecting maintenance programmes for premises. They are often put in charge of works being undertaken at a particular building site or they represent clients in property claims for compensation.

Training and professional structure

Entrants to the profession first obtain a degree or diploma which is accredited by the Royal Institution of Chartered Surveyors. There are approximately 70 institutions who offer such an accredited course. It is then necessary to undertake an assessment of professional competence, entrants being required to keep a diary. This stage usually lasts two years, after which the assessment and an interview take place. Those qualified in this way may use the initials 'ARICS'. Fellows of the Institute use the designation 'FRICS' and attain this qualification by being in a senior position for twelve years, or for five years with a postgraduate qualification, such as an MSc in surveying.

There are a number of divisions of surveying in terms of the work which surveyors do. Some operate in general practice as estate agents; others become quantity surveyors working on building sites, or as building surveyors advising on renovations; and yet others include those practising in the field of mineral surveying, land surveying and in rural practice.

Whether to use a surveyor or not will depend very much on the transaction concerned. It would be very unwise to undertake major building work or to purchase expensive property without using the services of a surveyor.

Surveyors will undertake a managing role for large construction projects, coordinating the other professionals on the team, including architects, builders and others. Ensuring that a firm is chosen which has wide experience of such a role should assist in ensuring the smooth running of the project. It is always preferable to have one firm or individual in charge in such large construction projects in order to ensure that project management is adequately carried out.

In many cases, using the surveying firm for this role is the most sensible decision, as few companies employ individuals with either the time available or the relevant skills to do the job themselves. This does not mean that surveyors should be let loose without any control. First, ensure that the contractual position is adequately covered and respective responsibilities are clear, and then have regular progress meetings to keep a check on how the development or project is proceeding. Where the project management is not being adequately carried out, make sure that problems are aired as early as possible so that a resolution can be achieved.

ARCHITECTS

Architects prepare plans and design buildings and other structures, and advise on the choice of building materials. They also provide consultancy services for large property developments. A number of architects offer property management services and will supervise contractors, install building services and negotiate planning permissions. In building an extension to a house employing an architect is not always necessary. Where a competent local builder is engaged, he may be able to draw up the plans himself. However, those wanting an element of style and good design are wise to use an architect. Ensuring that proper attention is given to instructing the architect in what type of result is needed — not just aesthetically, but also practically

— assists in achieving a good relationship between the architect and client.

Training and professional structure

Those entering the architectural profession enrol at a school of architecture and undertake a first degree. This is then followed by one year in practice, followed by two more years of study whilst taking a post-graduate diploma. After that a further year is spent in practice and then qualifying examinations are taken.

Architectural practices are professional partnerships. The partners will be self-employed and various individuals will be employed by them to assist them in their work.

Architects are regulated by the Architects Registration Council of the United Kingdom (ARCUK) and many are members of the Royal Institute of British Architects (details in Appendix 2).

PATENT AND TRADEMARK AGENTS

Any company wishing to take out a patent should employ a patent agent. There is no legal reason why an individual or company cannot make its own application to the patent office, but in practice it is necessary to draw up a detailed specification for the patent. This is something which most companies will find very difficult to do, particularly to make sure that the claims to the invention in the patent are sufficiently broadly drawn to catch all possible applications for the invention. It will be necessary to check the 'prior art' and to establish that there has been no prior publication of the invention.

Companies wishing to take out a trademark could more easily do this themselves, though this is not recommended. Forms are available from the trade marks registry and a fee is paid with the return of the form. Generally, though, unless money is very tight, a trademark agent is best used. They will assist with advising on where, throughout the world, the trademark should be registered. Registered design protection can also be obtained through patent agents, though again, there is no requirement that agents be used. Registered designs protect the aesthetic appearance of articles. Protection is obtained for a limited period and purely functional objects will not receive registered protection, unless a patent is available. Copyright or design right protection may be available and no registration is needed for those rights, though companies should always seriously consider the stronger protection available through registration of a patent, trademark or design.

With both patents and trademarks, any company which intends to operate outside the UK, now or in the future, should ascertain and determine where it should apply for protection of its patent and trademark rights. The future protection of the business name, reputation and inventions of the company on which its commercial success is based could be jeopardised by failure to obtain the protection needed at the outset. The company will have to determine whether to take out a patent at the patent office in London, or whether to apply through the European patent office in Munich for patents to be designated in particular contracting states.

In general, in this area it is best to employ professionals, rather than attempt to obtain this type of protection yourself. You will always need to consider whether to take out this type of 'intellectual property' protection at all. Many companies choose not to apply for patents to protect their inventions. Patenting involves publishing to the world details of the invention. No one else in the country where there is protection can then make products using that invention without the risk of being sued for patent infringement. Patents are strong monopoly rights and even those people manufacturing similar products, unaware that such activity infringes the patent, are at risk of being sued for patent infringement.

However, having the right to sue and the means to sue are two very different questions. As patent litigation is not cheap, smaller companies rightfully can see the disadvantage in publishing their inventions and instead seek to ensure their protection by keeping them confidential. This may be cheaper, but the legal protection is obviously not as strong.

With trademarks, again there is no obligation to register. Registrations can be made for both trade names used in connection with goods and those used in relation to services provided. If no registration is made, then other companies could use the name even in your business area, though if they were 'passing off' their business as yours you may be able to sue them for the tort (wrongful act) of 'passing off'. Generally, registered trademark protection is preferable and trademarks, unlike patents, can be renewed indefinitely.

There will be application and renewal fees to pay whether or not an agent is used. If an agent is used, then he will be made responsible for ensuring that renewal fees are paid on time. This is important, as otherwise the rights can lapse.

Training and professional structure

There are approximately 1300 patent agents in the UK, most of whom have a scientific background, such as an engineering or science degree. Graduates then take the professional examinations of the Chartered Institute of Patent Agents and the Institute of Trade Mark Agents and gain entry to the Register of Patent Agents and the Register of Trade Mark Agents. Details of the institutes are given in Appendix 2. Many agents will also be European Patent Attorneys, having also passed the European Qualifying Examination. Increasingly, companies exploiting European markets make applications to the European Patent Office for patents, designating those countries in which protection is desired, rather than making individual national applications.

Individuals also undergo a period of training. It takes approximately three or four years to qualify. Agents operate as professional partnerships, employing staff, in the same way as other professionals. Some agents are employed by firms of solicitors or work within industry.

MERCHANT BANKERS

When do you need a merchant banker? Companies contemplating a public listing on the stock exchange or a major rights issue to shareholders will require the assistance of merchant banks. Fees are large, but the deals themselves usually involve significant sums. Holding a 'beauty parade' and having several potential firms compete on service and cost may ensure that some financial savings can be made.

As most deals will involve attempting to persuade the public and institutions to invest, the use of an established, well regarded firm of merchant bankers can be essential. The merchant bankers will arrange the underwriting of the issue and liaise with the solicitors and accountants and other professionals on the team, preparing the prospectus for the issue and raising the funds required.

OTHER PROFESSIONAL SERVICE PROVIDERS

Banks

All companies use banks. Short of keeping all the firm's money in a drawer, there is little choice. This book does not discuss banks in detail, though banks do compete with other professionals for some services. Most high-street banks, for example, offer tax advisory services and it will be worth investigating whether the advice is cheaper than that offered by your accountant or specialist tax solicitor.

There is no need to describe in detail the services which banks provide, of which most people are aware. Ensuring that the bank charges which are levied on your account are clear, and the overdraft or other loan interest rate is established, will assist in ensuring that there are no difficulties between bank and customer later.

Bank charge 'checkers'

Some organisations offer to examine the bank statements of companies to check for errors and retain a percentage of the savings which result. Such professionals, paid on results, fulfil a worthwhile function, unless yours is a company employing staff who are sufficiently attentive to detail to examine each bank statement in order to check for errors, or you have such trust in the accuracy and competence of your bank that you do not believe that substantial mistakes are likely to have been made.

Stockbrokers

Stockbrokers are not dealt with in this book as they are principally concerned with investing funds of individuals and institutions, such as pension funds and unit trusts, rather than offering business advice to companies or partnerships. However, many of the principles set out in this book concerning choosing a professional, maintaining a good relationship and negotiating charges apply equally to stockbrokers as to other professionals. Determining, so that it is clear to both parties, exactly what freedom the stockbroker will have to invest on your behalf will ensure that problems are reduced. Even where the stockbroker is largely entrusted to take all investment decisions concerning a particular portfolio, keep a check on how the investments are going and change brokers if you are not satisfied.

Factors

Other professionals include factoring companies, who 'take an assignment' or transfer of debts owed to the company and then make their profit through recovering money due from such debtors under outstanding invoices.

The company which engages the factoring company benefits through having immediate access to the cash previously unavailable being comprised in such debts. Whether to factor debts will be a decision for the company concerned. It may be preferable to forego 100 per cent of debts outstanding in return for a smaller percentage for assurance that money is paid and for the early receipt of such money. Companies who generally have no problem with cash flow and bad debts, however, would do better to avoid factoring their debts in this way. It can put customers off.

This is merely one example of other types of professional and illustrates the necessity of ensuring that a reputable company is employed.

Most industries will have their own industry-specific professionals, who may not be included by name in this book. However, the general principles set out here will be applicable to those professionals, whatever their role.

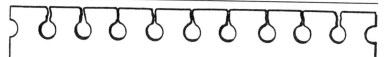

CHECKLIST

- Many different kinds of people are called 'professionals', including accountants, solicitors, barristers, management consultants, marketing and advertising advisers, surveyors, architects, patent and trademark agents

- Most are required to pass professional examinations and work their way up in their chosen profession from the role of trainee to employee, then to partner

- There can be some overlap between the respective roles of the different professionals

- Insurance may be available for some costs of professional advisers, such as legal expenses insurance

- Consider using a firm to check your bank charges or a factoring company to improve cash flow

3
Choosing and engaging a professional

We trust our health to the physician, our fortune and sometimes our life and reputation to the lawyer and attorney. Such confidence could not safely be reposed in people of a very mean or low condition. Their reward must be such as may give them that rank in the society which so important a trust requires.

Adam Smith, 1776

If you are buying a house you do not instruct a leading firm of solicitors charging rates of £250 per hour. Nor, if you are preparing your company for a public listing, do you use Joe Bloggs & Co, a high-street practitioner. This section will look at how to choose the right professionals and how best to instruct them.

GOLDEN RULES

Rule 1
Establish what work you need doing

The clearer you are on what work you need done, the better for everyone. Is it an annual audit of your accounts or the setting up of an offshore trust and tax avoidance scheme? If you have a hazy idea that you need a lawyer or accountant, is that correct? Be more specific. Is it necessary to instruct anyone at all? A small bad debt may be cheaper to write off than pursue, or you may be able to issue proceedings yourself with Citizens' Advice Bureau or Law Centre assistance. There may be better ways of recovering sums due. Have lunch with the managing director of the company with whom you are in dispute. Try all avenues.

However, there will be many occasions where professionals more than pay for themselves. Management consultants will cast a fresh eye over important areas of your business, resulting in substantial saving of costs. Professionals do not need to be there as a last resort, a necessary evil. The best solicitor or accountant will be a business adviser rather than simply telling you what the rules are. Bringing professionals in too late can cost more in the long run. Often an initial telephone conversation before the start of a deal saves money later.

If you have a contract to draft ring the lawyers for initial ideas on the types of issues you need to consider. It is no good calling them the day before you hope to sign a contract and ask them to give it a quick vet. It will not necessarily save you money. Did you consider indemnities, exclusion of liability and what the consequences are of terminating the agreement? Probably a major legal issue was missing and you are back to the negotiating table embarrassingly late.

An early discussion can result in the solicitor sending an office precedent or checklist giving you ideas from which to work. There may be tax-efficient ways of structuring a deal. Calling the accountants or tax lawyers at the stage when the terms of the deal are almost written in stone may be too late.

Rule 2
Consult early

Remember you are the client. Call the professional early, but make it clear what is expected. If you are a new client the professional will be particularly keen to do the work. Say that you want to talk through the issues and you will be going back to the professional when there is a document to prepare or consider. Whet his appetite. Make him want to do this work. Your conversation should leave it clearly established as to:

• whether you are instructing him;

- whether you pay for the telephone call;
- what the professional is to do after the call.

WHEN YOU NEED A PROFESSIONAL AND HOW TO FIND ONE

This all presupposes that you already have a professional to consult or know whom to instruct. The type of professional you require will usually be self-evident. If you need accounts auditing, you will require an accountant. If you want advice on improving the efficiency of your production line, you will need a management consultant. For a legal matter, a solicitor is needed.

Always consider carefully which type of professional to use. There may be circumstances in which your accountant will involve himself in advising on quasi-legal matters or your solicitor in giving tax advice. However, although many members of both professions are well able to advise, the particular individual may not be an expert, but just be zealously guarding his client. Ask exactly what experience that individual has of handling that type of matter, and at least question whether the matter should not really be handled by another type of professional more usually associated with that type of work.

Roll on the day of 'one-stop shopping' may be the wish of many who encounter so many different sets of professional fees to pay. But remember that you are paying for expertise and in the long run it may be cheaper to use three types of professionals who can all advise quickly and competently on the aspects with which they deal on a weekly basis.

Many individuals and companies are not sure how to go about finding a professional. This chapter gives advice on how to go about finding a professional for the type of work which you require to have done.

Personal recommendation

Personal recommendation is the best way to find a professional. Sound out your friends and competitors, but bear in mind, with competitors, that the professional's rules of conduct probably preclude him from acting for both you and your competitor on the same transaction. Whom do people you know use for the same type of work? It is no good using the accountant with whom you play golf, who runs a high-street practice, if you want advice on complex arrangements of which he has no experience. Make sure that the person who is recommending someone is aware of your requirements. Bloggs & Co may be excellent in one area, but completely inexperienced in another.

One way to discover whom your competitors are using for accountants is to look at their annual report and accounts which must be filed at Companies House for registered companies. These accounts are required by law to state the names and addresses of the accountants employed in the audit.

A word of warning if you personally are asked for a 'recommendation'. It is generally advisable not to 'recommend' anyone, in case they prove disastrous and your 'friend' chooses to hold you responsible for the recommendation. Much better to say, 'I have used X & Co in the past and have always had a good service, although I would never go so far as to recommend any firm'.

Professional bodies

If personal recommendation fails, then calling the relevant professional body may produce a response. The addresses, telephone and fax numbers of the relevant professional bodies are given in Appendix 2.

1. Solicitors are represented by the Law Society.
2. There are a number of accountancy bodies which represent accountants, including the Institute of Chartered Accountants of England and Wales, the Institute of Chartered Accountants in Scotland, the Chartered Institute of Certified Accountants and the Chartered Institute of Management Accountants.
3. Management consultants (as seen in Chapter 2) are involved in many fields of expertise. Appendix 2 sets out some of the organisations of which they may be members. There is also the Management Consultancies Association, which repre-

sents the largest consultancies in the UK (about 65 per cent of the market). The Institute of Management Consultants is another organisation which represents about 3300 consultants.

4. The surveyors' professional body is the Royal Institution of Chartered Surveyors.
5. Patent and trademark agents are represented by the Chartered Institute of Patent Agents and the Institute of Trade Mark Agents.
6. Most architects are represented by the Royal Institute of British Architects. All architects must register with the Architects Registration Council of the United Kingdom, though not all are members of the RIBA.
7. Barristers are represented by the General Council of the Bar.
8. Other professionals will all have relevant bodies of which they may have membership. Financial advisers will need to belong to one of the recognised supervisory bodies, such as LAUTRO.

Claimed specialisations and examinations

One difficulty which many encounter is that not all professional bodies are able to give information about which of their members specialise in a particular area. Some moves are afoot to allow professionals to claim areas of specialisation. In November 1992 the Council of the Institute of Chartered Accountants approved the circulation of a document to its members suggesting additional qualifications to reflect members' respective expertise in areas such as taxation, financial management and information technology.

Similar discussions have occurred within the solicitors' profession. In some areas, such as insolvency and taxation, professionals can sit an additional examination in order to become an insolvency practitioner or taxation expert (Associate or Fellow of the Institute of Taxation). Professionals may have recognised qualifications which show that at least they were able to pass an examination in a particular specialised area. Chapter 2 sets out some of the qualifications which management consultants might hold, for example in psychology or the personnel field. With management consultants there is no regulatory restriction on claiming a specialisation. Indeed, as they cover such a broad range it is only fair to the client for such consultants to clarify the areas in which they offer consultation. For further information regarding professional qualifications in specialised areas, consult the relevant directory. A selected list of reference material is given in Appendix 5.

Other organisations

Some organisations, such as the British Franchise Association, hold lists of solicitors who are experienced in the relevant area of law, such as in this case franchising law. Your own industry body may offer similar services or point you in the right direction when you are seeking professional advice possibly relevant to your industrial sector.

The big names and kudos

There may be a good commercial reason why you need a big city firm as your professional adviser. Before choosing firms, always consider carefully whether this aspect is a factor. Choosing a regional or less well-known firm may not enhance your company's reputation as much as might an association with a leading practice. When you seek to impress others in your accounts, or on a prospectus or other public document, by having a top name, or wish to frighten the competition or those whom you might sue by engaging the firm with the national reputation, then choosing a well-known firm may be the best option, following the direction that no one was ever fired for making the safe choice.

However, always analyse your reasons carefully and make sure that your choice can be commercially justified.

Advertisements

Many professionals advertise their services, either in the trade or national press, particularly when the press is running a special feature on their area of competence, or they do so more subtly through sponsorship of events, giving lectures and seminars, and mailing newsletters or other publications. In the past many professional bodies prevented their members from advertising their services and there are still restrictions on some forms of advertising. For example, solicitors are not allowed to 'cold call' potential clients, though mailings are permitted. Accountants have been allowed to advertise since 1984.

Although a firm is unlikely to risk advertising its services in an area in which it has no experience, most professional firms, unlike companies buying and selling products, do not need to advertise in this way in order to draw business. It can be that a firm is trying to break into a new area by launching an advertising campaign. So be sceptical of commercial advertisements and regard them as a last resort, or simply as a means of backing up a decision already taken to appoint a particular firm.

Firms which 'advertise' by means of giving lectures, writing articles and books should not be viewed with such scepticism. Such activities are usually a good indication of competence in the relevant area, whereas a paid advertisement simply indicates that the firm has sufficient funds to pay for the advertisement.

Company Z has recently been set up and needs a firm of accountants to prepare its accounts and offer assistance in determining and mitigating its tax liability. Mr Y is the managing director and he has had little experience of accountancy practices. He has heard of one of the international accountancy practices, who have been advertising heavily in the trade publications which he reads. He decides to instruct them. He is astounded when he receives his first bill.

He thought he could not go wrong by choosing such a practice, but the firm allocates a very junior member of staff to deal with Company Z's affairs. The individual does not seem to know what he is doing and, in fact, because of the nature of the products with which Company Z deals and its relationship with other group companies, its tax affairs are quite complicated. Eventually, very disillusioned, Mr Y calls up a friend in the industry who recommends a local firm, with very low overheads and young, keen, enthusiastic staff, who take over Company Z's affairs with alacrity and provide a very good value for money service. Mr Y is still arguing with the original firm over its bill.

Appointing auditors

The role of the auditors of a limited company is to check the financial information shown by the company's records so as to give an opinion on the accounts. This is principally for the protection of shareholders. All companies, except dormant companies, must appoint auditors as the law currently stands.

There are special legal rules concerning the appointment of auditors. Auditors are appointed at the annual general meeting when the accounts are presented to shareholders. Auditors hold office until the next annual general meeting. When auditors are appointed for the first time, the directors may make the appointment until the first annual general meeting at which accounts are laid before the members. It is also possible, if an 'elective resolution' has been passed, for the members to opt out of the annual appointment of auditors, the current auditors continuing in office until such time as they or the members wish them to leave. The fees paid to auditors are fixed by the company at the general meeting, too.

Only members of the ICAEW and CICA (details in Appendix 2) may be appointed as auditors. Auditors must be 'registered auditors', ie individuals properly regulated and with at least three years of practical training, most of it spent in auditing work. The following cannot be appointed as auditors:

1. Employees or directors or other officers of the company.
2. Employees and officers of holding or subsidiary companies and their employees or partners.
3. 'Connected' individuals, such as where the company to be audited is controlled by a member of the auditor's family or where the auditor has a financial interest in the company.

MAKING THE CHOICE

Names

You have a list of names of firms and want to proceed with instructing one. This may seem like a long process, but there is nothing to be gained in skimping on the question of choosing the right professional. It will save you money later and ensure that you are speaking to someone who knows about the area of work you wish him to do. If you simply want your house conveyed, then it may be adequate to look in your local paper or *Yellow Pages* and telephone round for quotes, but even there it is preferable if you can use someone whom a friend has used before. You want a firm which is quick and efficient and good value for money.

Obtaining some names should be possible very quickly if time is short, as information can be obtained over the telephone and firms can be telephoned that day. If speed is an important factor then explain that to the professional. If he is interested in doing the work for you, then he will pull out all the stops to accommodate your timetable. If he offers you an appointment several weeks hence, then move to the next professional on your list. If he is too busy to see you, this may indicate that he is very good at his job (he probably is), but that is of no use to you if you can never get any advice out of him when you want it.

It is reasonable to expect, in these days of the fax machine, a response to your letter within a day of receipt even if just by way of an acknowledgement, with a proposed timetable for a substantive response. Do not expect anything less. How quickly you should expect a substantive response depends on the nature of the query. Many good professionals will work all night if a job is particularly important and time is sensitive. If your professional won't, find one who will.

Armed with your list of names, telephone the firms concerned. It is clearly preferable if you have the names of the people within those firms who do the type of work in which you are interested. If not, then ask as clearly as possible for whoever is responsible for 'new audit business', or 'quality management consulting' or 'will drafting', or whatever. Make it clear that you are a potential new client and even the dullest of switchboard operators ought to give you some priority and have some notion to whom you should speak.

The first call

Once you are speaking to the right person, introduce yourself clearly and confidently. Do not spend too long describing your firm or your wonderful products: the professional will be interested to know the nature of your problem, or the work you require to be done, so that he can establish whether or not you are indeed speaking to the right person. Do not outline the entire problem yet: he will also want to have some idea of the size of your company or the money at stake in a deal. Is it a big or a small job? This is a question you would ask yourself in undertaking any new work and the professional is quite understandably similarly interested. In due course, sending your latest Annual Report and Accounts will help the professional get to know you.

However, you have yet to decide if this is the firm for you. Depending on how much work you are likely to put their way, it is recommended that you have an initial meeting before you decide to instruct a firm.

Rule 3
Arrange a pre-instruction meeting

'Beauty parades'

Solicitors, accountants, management consultants and other professionals increasingly spend time preparing for and undergoing 'beauty parades' these days, before being instructed. What is a beauty parade? Well, it is more than how they look, though smartly dressed, efficient-looking individuals are more likely to make a good impression on you. It is simply a meeting held before you give any work to the firm, when you can hear about the firm and they can hear about your company and the work that you need done. It should not be treated as an opportunity to get some free advice without paying for it and you should not expect the professional to advise you, other than to indicate areas in which they are competent to help you which are relevant to your problem.

When should you consider holding a beauty parade? Generally, you should hold one if you propose to appoint a firm to look after all your interests in a particular area, such as new corporate lawyers or new auditors or trademark agents, or for one transaction which is a large job, such as a takeover of a business or a large refinancing of the business. If you simply want a contract looked at for under £750 and there may never be any further work, then it is probably asking too much to expect your chosen professional to have a meeting for which he will not be paid and from which only a small amount of work will ensue. If there is going to be a steady stream of such contracts, however, then such an initial meeting is still recommended.

Increasingly, professionals are having to spend more and more time convincing potential clients that they should come to them and are used to preparing for and making presentations to clients. You, the client, can specify how you want such a meeting to proceed. The whole point of having a beauty parade is that it enables you to hear about a firm before giving them work.

Rule 4
See more than one firm

Although it may seem easier to visit only one firm, it is much better if you can make a comparison between at least two. For this purpose, seeing two or three firms over a period of a fortnight, or whatever timescale your other business commitments allow, enables you to decide which firm is right for you. It is a good idea to tell the firm that you are seeing other firms and name them if you wish. That should make them keener to get your business. You may like to leave it to the firm as to how they structure the session as that in itself may show you something about them — whether they are organised, too formal, too laid-back, uninterested and so forth.

However, do let them know how much time you have available. One hour is probably the optimum time. It is difficult to spend much longer talking about one's firm than that, no matter how wonderful one thinks it is, but allow an hour and a half in your schedule. If this is mid-morning, establish whether you will be rushing off or whether you could fit in lunch. The firm will probably pick up the tab, but do not assume that this will be the case and do not feel obliged to accept lunch: you may feel it pressures you morally into making a choice of that firm over the others you are seeing.

Inform the firm exactly who will be coming from your company. Probably three people at the most should go, but only send one if you wish; two is more usual. Present someone senior and the individual who will most often be contacting the professional. Give their job description and title in writing and ask who the firm will be putting forward. Explain the purpose of the meeting as far as you are concerned: that you need to choose a firm and are considering them, that you would first like to know more about them and are seeing several other firms.

At the meeting you may be presented with a series of rehearsed talks. Many professionals employ PR agents these days and attend public speaking courses. Do not be afraid to interrupt and ask questions. You are all likely to get on much better if the ice is broken and discussion ensues, rather than sitting looking at some rather uninspiring slides which leave your main questions unanswered. Questions you should ask are:

1.   What work have they done in this area before?
They may be constrained by professional rules from naming clients, though some will happily mention companies for whom it is a matter of public record that they act or who have consented to being named. However, they can in any event describe transactions of a similar nature, even if no names are given. You might like to ask the odd technical question.

2.   What other work do they do?
Although many companies now use particular firms for different types of work, your company may be small enough to make it easier and, in the long run, cheaper to place all your work with one practice. You may need them to do work in other areas later. If you do want to hear about types of work other than your main concern, then it is considerate to tell the firm in advance so that they can have present their expert in that area of work.

3.   What will it cost?
You may like to save this question till the end, but it should not be forgotten. There is no reason why you should be coy about this issue: if you were having your washing machine repaired or plumbing fixed, you would make sure you had a quote in

advance. Professionals are used to talking about fees these days and if they will not discuss that issue, then maybe they are not the firm for you. Ask them:

(a)   What are their hourly charging rates, if any, for different levels of staff?

(b)   What level of fee earner or employee would be doing the work?

(c)   How often are bills sent out?

(d)   Would they be prepared to give you an estimate for each job which you send them?

(e)   Would they consider a monthly retainer?

(f)   When are their rates reviewed?

(g)   Would they consider discounting on their rates if you were to become a client? Many firms offer discounts on their rates. Do not assume that the rates are not negotiable. (There is more about charging in Chapter 4.)

4.   How does the firm operate?
Is there one partner or other senior person responsible for your work and who will do the day-to-day work?

5.   Do they have other clients in your industry?
They may be very familiar with an area of practice, but have given advice to companies only in one narrow industrial sector. A firm which knows companies in your industry will give a better service. Firms acting almost solely for companies in the information technology sector may be very hot on patenting computer hardware inventions, but may not have experience in patent litigation for industrial machines.

6.   Everything you need to know.
Tell them as much as possible about your company, but do not turn the session into you addressing them. You have come along to hear what they have to say and to be convinced, or otherwise, that they are the right firm for you. Take notes of relevant points and let them know how quickly you will come back to them with your decision. This will depend on who else you are seeing and the urgency of the job.

7. Are they completely independent?

Most professional partnerships will be independent. Accountants and solicitors will not be in the pay of other organisations,
although it does no harm to ask questions about what industry
groups or competitors of yours they also represent and whether
those other bodies would have a problem with them acting for
you, too. However, some consultants will have links with other
companies and will be trying to sell you products as well as
offering advice. Although members of the Institute of Management Consultants and Management Consultancies Association
are not permitted to have such links, many other consultants
will represent third parties. Whether you would wish to employ
such consultants will very much depend on the premium you
place on obtaining independent advice. Most companies would
feel more comfortable in the knowledge that their consultant is
going to recommend that they purchase products from the best
supplier on the market, without his choice being influenced by
commission or any other payment which he might receive
through recommending the company with which he is connected.

If you are seeing other firms, then try to ensure that at least one
person from your team is present at all the interviews so that
you can have some consistency and at least one person will be
able to undertake a fair comparison. Ask for the firm's brochure,
if it has one, and any other relevant materials and leaflets which
it produces.

For a beauty parade, it is preferable to go to the professional's
office so that you can observe the professionals on their home
ground. Subsequently, it is a good idea to invite the professionals to come to you at least once to show them around,
though when meetings are necessary later on it is generally
cheaper to go to them.

Do you like the professional?

You have found professionals in the discipline in which your
needs lie. You believe them to be experts in their field and have
met members of the firms from which you are choosing. How do
you make your choice? You will have your own priorities: you

may be looking for someone with whom you will be working closely, so ensuring that you will be able to relate well to each other may be of paramount importance. In that case, ask yourself if you liked the people you met. Despite the adage that opposites attract, generally people of similar background and personality find it easier to relate to each other. Did you feel there was such convergence during the meeting, or from any other background information which you possess about the individuals with whom you would be working?

Did you leave the meeting thinking that the individuals fielded by the firm were people with whom you would be happy to do business? Alternatively, did you feel indifferent to them or even have a feeling of dislike? The difficulty is that a short meeting cannot give you much of an insight into individuals and how they behave in a different environment. You will not be able to subject your professionals to psychological testing, as you might to an individual seeking employment with your company. However, if you feel you are generally a good judge of people, then follow your instinct if it really is important to you to like those with whom you work.

In considering this factor it is vital to know who will be doing your work. The firm may have fielded its brightest and best rising stars, but this is no good to you if they will not actually be undertaking your work. You want to meet the people with whom you would be dealing on a day-to-day basis. Make this clear before you arrange the beauty parade. You may want guarantees, particularly for work such as consultancy, where individuals may be working from your premises for a significant period of time, that the individuals named will indeed work for you throughout.

Some individuals, members of professional partnerships, are hopeless at beauty parades of this sort; they stammer, blush, have nothing to say or say too much. The firm concerned may be aware of this and ensure that such people never attend these sessions. Indeed, they may employ individuals who spend a large proportion of their time doing presentations of the sort considered here. Although such people may be very competent at telling you all you need to know about the firm concerned, they are not the people with whom you will be working and their slick presentation may make it harder for you to draw out the faults of the practice. By asking probing questions before and during the beauty parade, you should be able to find out whether or not this is the case. Simply ask whether the individuals concerned do many such presentations and how the firm structures such sessions. Do they use outside professional help? Make it clear that you will want to meet the people who will be supervising, and the individuals who will actually be undertaking your work, if you do choose the firm under consideration.

Do they cost too much?

Cost may be your most important consideration. Do not just go by what you were told at the interview. Wait until you have received a letter of engagement, or other written terms of business, which set out the cost estimate, if this factor is particularly important for you. The discussion of cost at the beauty parade may not have been as thorough as it should have been. There may be hidden extras. Ensure that in making any cost comparison, you are comparing like with like. Chapter 4 considers charging in more detail.

In making a cost comparison, ensure that you are making a fair choice. If the professional refused to estimate costs, then consider why. Will you be able to operate your business without knowing the likely cost of professional advice for which you need to budget? Perhaps not. On the other hand, do not always assume that cheapest is best; like everything else, you get what you pay for. However, professional fees do vary and some firms have not adjusted rates to reflect economic circumstances in the same way as others have. If cost is important to you, say so at the presentation and ensure that you receive an estimate.

Do they know their stuff?

Expertise is probably the factor which ought to be highest up your list of priorities in picking professionals. This is really what you are paying for and unfortunately you cannot assume that just because an individual has passed the required professional examinations, he will be as good and knowledgeable as any other. How do you judge expertise and knowledge at the presentation? This can be difficult, particularly because it is not the usual function of the presentation to advise you then and there concerning the problem in relation to which you are seeking their professional advice.

Using the methods recommended earlier in this chapter, on speaking to others within the industry and looking at relevant guidebooks, should ensure that an informed choice is made. Do not believe everything the professionals themselves tell you. They want your work, and in the same way that you might reassure a customer that there will be no problem in fulfilling an order when that might not be strictly accurate, some professionals may be at the least economical with the truth. The best will tell you when what you require is outside their field and inform you about other firms who might be able to help you. This practice should ensure that you will consider the orginal firm in the future, when there is some work within their sphere.

There is no harm in asking questions at the presentation; look into the area with which you are concerned and ask questions. Do not be fobbed off with refusals to answer; such a refusal may mask a lack of knowledge. Put a detailed question to each person present, if possible. You may, however, not know enough about the area in which you are seeking advice to pose any such questions at all. Try, in those circumstances, to find out more about other similar matters or clients with whom the firm is involved. Listen out for phrases such as: 'It's all a bit too technical to explain here', 'It's a while since I looked at that', 'Mrs Jones, who unfortunately couldn't be with us today, handles that', 'I leave all the detail to the youngsters fresh from college'.

Is it the right sort of firm?

You are likely to have come to a decision about the type of firm you wish to instruct before you get as far as attending a presentation or beauty parade. The presentation will be made by a number of firms of similar size. However, that may not be the case; firms, large and medium-sized, can often provide equally good and efficient service. You may use the presentation as an opportunity to decide what size of firm to use, and also whether you wish to use a general practice type of firm or one that specialises only in the area in relation to which you need advice. If you are likely to require advice in other areas and would wish to use the same firm for that, then a firm that can fulfil all your requirements would be better. However, as mentioned above, many companies now use different firms for different types of work and some even use a range of firms or a panel of approved firms for the same type of advice, effectively requiring them to compete with each other, not only for the initial advice, but also for each piece of work which requires outside advice or assistance.

You may decide to give work to both, or even all, the firms whom you see. If so, tell them; and it is also preferable to tell them the names of the other firms with whom they will be competing. If you need to choose one firm from several different types or sizes of practice seen at the presentation, then bear in mind the greater financial resources of the larger firms. They are more likely to have overnight wordprocessing services and sophisticated computer systems, which may be able to connect with your own systems, so that documents could be transmitted by E-mail.

On the other hand, your small company may not be regarded as a particularly important client of a larger firm. You may feel happier with a firm which regards you as a great catch. You will get a feel for this at the presentation. Did everyone turn up on time? Is there a partner there? Has effort been put into impressing you? Have they gone to the trouble of researching your company? Do they appear interested?

Is the firm run and organised to suit your needs?

The presentation should result in your knowing how the firm operates. Do you like their structure? Do they assign you to one fee earner as your point of contact? Will you see a range of people? It may not be appropriate that you do, but it is certainly a factor you should consider. Did they tell you how they handle correspondence? How fast do you think they operate? What technology do they use? What do their buildings look like? That last question can be a matter of personal taste. Some excellent professional firms have not spent vast amounts of money on their offices; it is your money they would be spending, in any event! Others have spent large sums as an indication of their commitment to their practice. Pleasant working conditions can improve performance of staff and you may be bringing your own clients or companies with whom you may be doing deals to their offices.

It will be your personal preference as to how important these factors are. What you must ensure is that you know something about the firms from whom you are choosing, whether they are big or small, who runs them, who supervises whom, how they operate their relationship with clients, whether they offer regular newsletters as part of their services or seminars which you can attend without cost.

So, the choice is yours. Remember that professionals are not appointed under long-term contracts of fixed periods. They may be engaged to do one job, but other pieces of work do not have to be put their way. You are at liberty to change the professional. If you find that you have made the wrong choice, then instruct another professional in their place. Chapter 6 describes how to go about sacking a professional.

APPOINTING A PROFESSIONAL

When you have chosen a firm to act for you, this should be set out in writing. Indeed, many professional bodies require or advise their members to set out the terms of business in a letter to the new client. The Law Society's Practice Rule 15 requires that clients know the name and status of the person responsible for the day-to-day conduct of a matter and the 'principal' responsible for its overall supervision. A letter summarising the 'retainer' between solicitor and client is recommended. In the Law Society's Legal Practice Directorate's booklet, *Client Care — a Guide for Solicitors*, sample letters of 'appointment' for contentious (litigation) and non-contentious business are given.

Most solicitors now issue such a letter to a new client. It would normally cover:

- who is responsible for the work and the partner in overall charge;
- details of how fees are calculated (more details on fees are given in Chapter 4);
- whether any money is required in advance on account of costs, and when bills are rendered and payment expected;
- to whom any complaints should be directed.

If your new solicitor does not send you any such letter, suggest to him that it would be in both your interests to have such matters set out in writing. Be warned if no such letter is forwarded. If your action does not prompt a letter, then write to him yourself, setting out what you regard as the terms between you and leave it to him to object. You should expect him to inform you of the likely timescale for completion of the matter, what is the next step to take the matter forward and what action is required by you, if any. Appendix 3 includes a pro forma of a letter you could use as a basis for your own letter. This may be modified to suit the particular professional concerned and the type of job. If he has given you an estimate over the telephone or explained at the initial meeting who will undertake the work within the firm, then simply include that in your letter.

Even when you receive a letter in these terms, if he does not summarise what you have asked him to do, then a letter sent back from you acknowledging your acceptance of the terms and stating what you have asked him to do on your behalf should help to avoid misunderstandings later.

The Institute of Chartered Accountants in its Members' Handbook (obtainable from the ICAEW, details in Appendix 2) provides that ICAEW member accountants should likewise issue a letter of engagement, which should include a section concerning how fees are calculated — on the time spent, the skills and responsibilities of the partners and fee earners involved — and also setting out when bills are rendered and when they are due. As with solicitors, if your accountant does not send you such a letter, then request one and in any event confirm your instructions in writing.

The Royal Institution of Chartered Surveyors leaves it up to its members whether or not there is a letter of engagement, although it does recommend that it is always sensible to have a written agreement. The Professional Conduct Rules are obtainable from the RICS (see Appendix 2). The Regulations provide that a member acting for a seller of property shall 'when accepting instructions, notify his client of the terms and conditions, including conditions relating to his charges and the payment of expenses, on which he is to act', unless the client is already aware of the conditions. To inform the client orally would still comply with this rule, of course.

The Royal Institute of British Architects' Rule 1.1 requires that members, when undertaking an engagement — whether by a contract of engagement or the supply of services — should define and record the terms agreed, including the scope of the service, the allocation of responsibilities and any limitation of liability, the method of calculation of remuneration and the provision for termination. Technically there could be an oral arrangement with the architect, the architect recording in the file the terms reached. In most cases, a letter between the parties would be the easiest way to comply with the rule.

Patent Agents' professional rules do not specify that a letter of engagement be issued or fees estimated. Instead, it is left up to members, although their Professional Conduct Rules do specify that they should not charge unjustified fees.

You can see, then, that virtually all professional bodies recommend to their members in one way or another that the terms of engagement be set out.

Some types of engagement, such as for management consultants, merit a formal contract or at least a very clear letter setting out the work to be undertaken. As well as addressing the issues mentioned earlier in this section, the letter should cover:

- how the work will be judged complete, such as what the final report will address;
- what expenses the consultant can incur in performing his duties;
- where the consultant will be based and what demands he can place on your staff;
- when the consultant should finish the task;
- whether the consultant will supply goods or will be entirely

independent and, if the consultant is to act as an agent on behalf of your company, what powers he will have in that capacity.

Rule 5
Insist on a letter of engagement from the professional

Armed with the terms on which you will operate, the work can go ahead. Before proceeding with consideration of the ongoing relationship between you and your professional, the vexed issue of fees, dealt with in Chapter 4, needs to be addressed.

THE IN-HOUSE PROFESSIONAL

There will come a stage in the development of all businesses beyond a certain size when they will consider whether it would not be better to employ a professional within the practice. Advice will be 'on tap' and the employee will know the ins and outs of the business. When this will be appropriate will depend on the size of the demand for the type of professional service which that company has. If it rarely contacts professionals, then clearly there is no point in employing one; if there is a constant stream of work, then it may make economic sense to have its own.

Some companies have recently cut back on in-house professionals in the recession, seeing them as an overhead which can be excised and buying in services as and when they are required. Some quite large companies have taken very different views concerning the size of their in-house legal departments, for example. A small nucleus of solicitors or barristers may be employed who coordinate the placing of work outside or, at the other extreme, in-house experts on a wide range of legal areas can be employed with little work being placed outside.

Which is best? The in-house lawyer is usually a generalist, with, of course, notable exceptions. There seems merit, in times when the importance of minimising overheads has never been greater, in employing just a few in-house professionals only, or none if you are a small company, and then buying in expertise as and when it is needed. However, there is no doubt that employing professionals is much cheaper where there is a steady flow of work. Continuing with the example of solicitors, a solicitor with a few years' experience can be employed at a salary of around £30,000 (1993, London prices). Outside legal advice is unlikely to cost less than £100 per hour.

SUMMARY

Those choosing outside professionals should ensure that they amass as much information as possible before drawing up a short-list of at least three (preferably up to six) professionals to arrange to meet. Ensuring that the presentation is a two-way process, allowing you, the client, to elicit the information which you need to make an informed choice of professional firm, should result in a choice based on the best information available. There will always be an element of trust in the relationship between professional and client, in that the professional alone has the detailed knowledge, so the client does not know what is missing and cannot judge if the advice is right or comprehensive. Professional bodies and examinations ensure that, on the whole, a basic level of competence is obtained, but much the best way to find a good professional is to use an individual (not just a firm) recommended by someone whom you know and respect.

CHECKLIST

- Determine what work needs to be done by a professional

- Consult early

- Find a professional through the personal recommendation of colleagues and friends, professional bodies, specialisations or extra examinations sat by the professional, guide books, advertisements

- Note the special rules on appointing auditors — at a company's AGM

- Arrange a 'beauty parade' or presentation by selected firms, at which you should ask pertinent questions about past experience, billing etc.

- Ensure that there is a letter of appointment setting out the work which has been agreed to be done, when it will be done, how much it will cost and who will undertake the work

- Consider, when your business reaches a size sufficient to justify the cost, employing an in-house professional adviser

4
Charging and how to obtain the best deal

'A profession' it has been well said, is a vocation founded upon specialised educational training, the purpose of which is to supply disinterested counsel and service to others, for a direct and definite compensation, wholly apart from expectation of other business gain.

Sidney and Beatrice Webb, 1917

Professional advice is expensive; whether it should be is another issue. This chapter will show you how to negotiate lower charges. There can be no doubt that the quality of the service is very important indeed and ensuring that you choose the right professional (as described in Chapter 3) should help you choose someone who is familiar with the area in which you need advice. But this does not mean that the price is unimportant.

Increasingly, companies are refusing to pay the huge charges levied with impunity by professional practices in the boom years of the 1980s. There is no cosy cartel of professionals. The market-place for professional services has become a ruthless, cut-throat place in the early 1990s, where firms, anxious to keep staff occupied rather than declare the redundancies which are now a regular feature of the professional scene, will accept work with very little potential profit indeed at the rates negotiated.

Many smaller companies and individuals are unaware of this change in emphasis and assume that they should pay the rates quoted to them. Whilst it is true that larger companies, who can assure a professional practice a certain fixed quantity of work each year, are in a better position to negotiate discounts on charging rates on, effectively, a 'discount for bulk' type of arrangement, there is no reason why smaller companies cannot agree reductions on charging rates also; and this chapter shows you how.

FEES

Professional charges can be very high indeed, with some London solicitors firms charging up to £450 per hour for advice. Many partners in London firms charge over £200 per hour. Accountants do not come much cheaper. In November 1992 a Gallup survey of 200 large to medium-sized UK companies showed that 57 per cent of companies using London law firms, and 48 per cent of all companies, thought that they were paying too much for legal advice. Accountants, in the same survey, were regarded as overcharging by 40 per cent of those surveyed.

Also in 1992, the *International Financial Law Review* published figures comparing the cost, again of lawyers, of US and UK firms, contrasting a US figure for a top Wall Street lawyer of $350 per hour with London firms at the equivalent of $585. The exchange rate has not helped this differential and US firms do charge for more separate items and more people working on each job, but still the comparison is not favourable.

Consultancy rates can presently be as high as £900 per day, ranging upwards from a figure of £250. There have been other public complaints about the issue of professional charges recently, with some complaining that charges have been increased in time of recession. PLCs are increasingly looking at ways of reducing professional costs, by novel methods such as caps, fixed fees and itemised bills. Large companies with considerable financial clout can be in a strong position to negotiate. It is often the small and medium-sized companies who simply accept the bills sent to them or the fees quoted.

There is no need: if one firm will not accept work from you at a reduced rate, another firm may well do so. The embarrassment factor can be at work in some companies' reluctance to discuss fees with their professionals. Just because the professional is not dressed in a blue overall and is engaged in the apparently high-minded pursuit of interpreting accounting standards or statutory instruments does not mean that he or she is above or beyond the question of costs.

You are buying services and are entitled to know what it will cost.

What you are paying for

What are you paying for in the typical professional fee? Usually the profit element in the fee is about 20 per cent. All the rest will be for overheads. The major overhead is salaries. Professional firms employ well-qualified professionals, graduates with post-graduate professional qualifications. Such individuals have become used to high salaries. There is a downward trend (in 1993) in such salaries, with, for example, some solicitors' practices paying newly qualified staff less than their counter-parts were receiving in the previous year. Such reductions are psychologically significant, as are the small pay rises and pay freezes which are commonplace in 1993, but it will take some time before they result in any significant reduction in the overheads of the professional firms concerned.

To reiterate, salaries are the principal overhead element. In addition firms have to pay for premises and it is here that savings can be made by choosing a regional rather than a London firm. The cost not only of premises, but also of salaries, is less in the provinces, which has led a number of major companies to place their work with regional practices. Some city firms rented expensive offices at the height of the property boom and are finding the excess space that they took impossible to let to other companies. Other overheads include the usual expenses of any business, such as paper, telephones, etc.

Generally, the partners in professional firms draw a notional salary of a fairly modest amount and then divide the firm's profits, if any, between them in the proportions which they have agreed. Partners in professional partnerships have had to accept much lower profit shares in recent years, but it is still the case that some partners draw sums of up to £1million per annum. These will be the exceptions, generally internationally renowned experts, who work extremely long hours and can demand fees commensurate with their international standing. It is certainly not unusual for partners in central London firms to earn a profit share of £100,000 to £250,000. However, many will then leave a major proportion of such earnings in the practice to pay for new buildings, computer systems, etc. Other professionals earn more modest amounts, in the £20,000 to £50,000 range.

The firm you employ may need to charge you high sums in order to maintain the expensive lifestyles of the partners. You may be better advised to go to a cheaper firm, provided the quality of service is as good.

ESTIMATES

Rule 1
Mention fees early on

There are experts in many professional fields and they will be expensive. You do not want to find yourself landed with a massive bill at the end of a transaction which you cannot pay and which is quite out of proportion to the value of the transaction itself or the project with which the professional has been involved. He may well be able to justify the bill and sue you for payment of it. **Find out first.**

If you have a smallish job and are just calling round for estimates then make sure that it is clear what the estimate is for. Most firms are accustomed to giving estimates these days and, as observed in Chapter 3, their professional rules may require them to give an estimate in any event. Solicitors are urged to give estimates, but are not yet obliged to do so. Most solicitors these days do give advance notice of costs and you should expect it. Those firms which have accepted the Law Society's published practice management standards are required to give costs information. The giving of a binding 'quotation' is unusual, as it can be extremely difficult to judge how much work will be involved in a transaction at the outset.

There has been a traditional reluctance by professionals to give details of fees, which is only slowly being overcome. Describe in as much detail as you can the transaction or the work which is likely to be involved. If the professional will not be pinned down to giving any figure at all, or just to giving the hourly rate without saying how many hours are likely to be spent, then make suggestions. How much will drafting the agreement cost? How much will attending the meeting cost, assuming it does not take longer than half a day? How much have they charged other clients with a similar type of work recently? That latter question will serve a two-fold purpose: it will draw out whether the professional has, in fact, done other work of this sort, and will also show what sort of level of fees are usually charged for work of that nature.

The stage to broach fees is at the outset.

Require the following:

- an estimate of what the work will cost;
- an assurance that you are informed as soon as the costs are nearly up to the level quoted and that no further work is done above the quoted figure until you have given consent and obtained a further estimate from the professional.

In this way you should not have too many shocks on the fees front.

Rule 2
Get the estimate in writing

Expect the estimate to be hedged around in caveats. The ingenuity of some professional firms in this field can be incredible. It is not an easy task giving a client an estimate for professional fees. The answer is often akin to 'How long is a piece of string?'. It can be impossible to predict how long a matter will take and many professional charges are based principally on the time spent on the matter. The other side in a transaction may accept an agreement which has been drafted exactly as it stands or there may be months of negotiation and meetings between all parties and their lawyers before the matter is resolved.

However, this is not to say that estimates are worthless. There is a psychological advantage in getting the professional to quote a cost. He is more likely to ensure that the job is done efficiently and that there is no duplication of work within the office. No sensible professional will be driven down on price to such an extent that the job is no longer cost-effective. Their professional rules ought to ensure that no compromise on quality is given at the expense of cost.

That may be the case in an ideal world, but you should be alert to the risk of driving too hard a bargain. It may be preferable to have quality and certainty in professional fees than skimping and rushing, with a poor job done. If it is obvious that you cannot afford to pay the fees being estimated to you, then perhaps the answer is to go to a regional firm rather than a London one, or to a high-street practice rather than a city centre practice.

If the estimate is in writing, there can be no doubt later about what the estimate was given for, or what figure was given: was it for the whole job, or up to a certain stage, was it suggested that the bill would be unlikely to exceed the figure quoted or was it very much a general, ball park figure which could well be exceeded? Having a written estimate lessens the risk of there being any dispute about the matter. If your professional does not write to you with details of an estimate given, or a revised or additional estimate later, then write to him yourself setting out your understanding of the situation. A sample of such a letter appears in Appendix 3.

Alternatively, if you really cannot afford the expert advice which you require, it may be possible to give the expert discrete parts of the work.

> **1. Get the other side to draft the agreement** (though
> this loses you control) **and have your lawyer give it a
> quick vet for major issues.**
> **2. Ask for advice on one aspect only, taxation, intellec-
> tual property issues or particular areas about which you
> are not sure.**

In reducing an audit fee, consider asking the auditor what steps
you could take the following year to reduce the fee and ensure
that you provide as much information as is necessary, rather
than require the auditor to spend considerable amounts of time
finding the information needed. Provide secretarial assistance
yourself and arrange to pay all the auditor's out-of-pocket
expenses so that they are not included on the bill.

There are inherent dangers in skimping too much, but some
advice will usually be better than none; if economic constraints
operate, then this approach could be adopted. Only individuals
on an extremely low income will be entitled to most forms of
legal aid, but always consider free business advice given by
Government small business agencies, the Department of Trade
and Industry and other state sources.

The Department of Trade and Industry subsidises the
provision of consultancy services to small businesses (employing fewer than 500 workers). Companies are only required,
under the Enterprise Initiative, to pay half of five to fifteen days'
worth of consultancy fees. There is a ceiling on the amount
which consultants can charge when part of the scheme. Details
are obtainable from the DTI. This scheme can significantly
reduce the cost of management consultants.

TIME COSTS

If you want to understand why fees are at the level they are then
some background information about how fees are fixed is
helpful. Most professional bodies set out rules about fees in

their codes of professional conduct, to which reference should be made for the full details. Relevant factors in setting fees include the complexity of the matter, its importance to the client, and the value of the transaction. Some consultants supply goods to the client as well as offering advice by way of the provision of consultancy services. They may make most of their fees through commission from the companies whose equipment they recommend. Some professionals charge principally on the basis of the value of the transaction.

However, the most frequently used indicator for charging is the time spent on the matter. Most firms charge principally on the time spent and keep computerised records of time spent on each client's business. The consequence of such time recording is that the professional is able to see how much time has been spent for a client and obviously, the more discussions between client and professional there are, the higher the fee. This is not to say that you should not communicate with your professional for fear of increasing the fee; communication can reduce fees. Keeping each other informed ensures that no work is undertaken which is unnecessary or superseded by events.

However, as soon as you are on the telephone to the professional, in many cases the stop-watch has started ticking at whatever the professional's charge-out rate is. Constantly pestering him with calls will not be the most efficient way of getting the work done. You should expect him to keep you regularly informed of how the matter is progressing, but do avoid unnecessary discussions. If you are aware that as soon as you ring or he receives your letter he will make a note, whether in a book or on a computer, of the time and duration of the work done, then you can seek to minimise time-wasting.

The time issue is emphasised here. Although time is not the only relevant element, it is the easiest one with which professionals work and is usually the pricing basis for the charge.

Time charging rewards the slow and inefficient.

This is why having a realistic estimate helps avoid the situation, particularly in a recession when professional firms are often not fully employed, where more time is spent on a matter than necessary. Parkinson's Law applies as much to professionals as to others. One piece of work can be expanded to fill an afternoon if there is nothing else to do. Where firms suffer from this problem, time may well be written off, but, even so, having the estimate in place should minimise the problem to an extent.

There will be circumstances where the work, for which an initial estimate has been given, subsequently transpires to be much more complicated than either you or the professional orginally thought. The professional should give you a revised estimate and also an explanation as to why there is more work to be done than originally anticipated.

Different levels of professionals will have different hourly charging rates. These will usually reflect the respective seniority of the people concerned. Senior partners will have a much higher rate than newly qualifieds or trainees. Ask for details of the rates of all who will be undertaking your work. Firms ought to have in place structures whereby junior members undertake the easier work, checking documents, basic audits and so on.

Rule 3
Ask the firm whether you really need a partner to do the work proposed — it may be perfectly competently handled by a more junior member of the firm

On the other hand, if you have an important transaction of your company you may prefer a partner to handle it. The junior may need to learn on the job. He may need to consult the partner frequently anyway and you could end up paying for both when the partner, who has done many such transactions before, could have done the job much more cheaply in the long run.

Rule 4
Ask whether the individual allocated to the job has done this type of work before — insist on a partner if you wish

KEEPING FEES LOW

You can reduce your professional bills by using the following tips.

Passing on all information

Give your professional all the information which he needs initially. Do as much of the work yourself as possible. It may be a nuisance for you to go through old papers summarising relevant facts, or setting out in a long letter the history of a matter, but at least it is at your expense. It will avoid him being obliged to ask you questions later or have you in for a meeting.

Clarify the respective roles of different professionals involved, so that duplication is avoided.

Meetings

Only meet when necessary. A lot can be achieved in a properly timed and planned meeting, but there is no doubt that meetings bump up costs. Particularly if you are asking the professional to travel to your premises or those of another party to the transaction, you will be paying not only for his time spent at the meeting, but also for his travelling time.

1. Let him know your corporate policy concerning travel expenses. You will be expected to pay his travel expenses, but if your own directors have to travel economy class there is no reason why your lawyer or accountant should not also.
2. Flying may seem more expensive for domestic meetings, but weigh up the respective cost of his hourly charging rate incurred if he is driving across the country against the air

fare. Almost always the quicker travel route, whatever the cost, will save you money. Also, if he flies or goes by rail he can work en route.

3. Arrange his travel for him if you are attending the meeting too, so you pay and have control over the arrangements. It will only appear on your bill later anyway, and you may have negotiated a better deal with hotels or your travel agents than he has.

4. Prepare an agenda for all meetings and stick to it. Meetings need a leader or time can pass very unprofitably. If there are intractable issues and no progress is being made, leave them to one side and deal with everything else.

5. Confirm before the arrangements are made that only he will be coming to the meeting. There may be occasions when a team is needed, but not always. If the partner is handling the matter then he can brief his assistants later. If the assistant is doing most of the work, perhaps he alone should attend the meeting. Only consent to attendance by more than one representative of the professional where the professional has made out a convincing case for the necessity for such attendance. If the assistant is just there to take a note of the meeting, suggest you have someone from your own company sitting in for this purpose or that you tape-record the session.

> **If more than one person attends a meeting, your costs may double.**

Months of negotiation can be successfully brought to fruition by a meeting with all the parties present. Ensure that both sides have present all the individuals, both outside professionals and those within the company, who will need to be consulted before a deal can be finalised. There is no point in attending a meeting with your accountant only to find that the other side have not brought theirs along and everything has to be checked by him before agreement is reached.

Timetables and who is responsible

Set out a timetable for the matter. Nothing puts up time costs more than transactions which take ages. The longer a building takes to finish or a project to complete, the greater the cost will be. Each time a matter is put on one side and later dusted off again, the professional has to reread the file and reacquaint himself with the matter.

> **You will be paying for the professional reacquainting himself with a matter that is left to lie dormant.**

Do not lose momentum. Set a timetable. Make it clear to all parties that there is no deal if agreement is not reached within a certain timescale. The timetable can be discussed in advance with the lawyers and accountants or other professionals involved. You may have a wholly unrealistic idea of how long it takes, for example, to dispose of a business. You may need to obtain consent from the Office of Fair Trading, which could delay the transaction for weeks. There could be all manner of legal and other matters which might hold up the deal. Consult about a draft timetable. Agree it and stick to it.

Once you have agreed a timetable with all the professionals involved, ensure that it is adhered to by all parties. Set it out in writing and make it your business to chase up members of the team who are dragging their feet.

> **The importance of having one individual within your company responsible for a matter cannot be over-emphasised.**

Shifting responsibility within a company delays matters greatly. The new person has to acquaint himself with the matter. He may have his own views on it and want a deal structured in a different way. Even worse is the situation where it is not clear at all who is responsible.

Tell your professional from whom to take instructions.

Channel all work to him through you or some other responsible individual. Central control ensures that you are able to keep a check on costs and enables one person to have an overview of all the services which your firm is obtaining from that professional. Even where this is impossible, ensure that you or the responsible individual is copied with correspondence passing between the professional and other parts of your company. Central control also ensures that momentum is maintained on a deal and it is completed as planned.

Concentrated working

Concentrated working is where a professional is undertaking a major task for a client, which involves him working almost full-time on a matter. This is expensive, but it is very cost-effective. There is no chance of the professional, involved in other matters, having to revise a file and remember what was involved. He will be fully involved in a transaction.

For these types of deals, the professional will be used to having to work through the evening and over the weekend. Do not be afraid of suggesting such arrangements and ensure that there will be adequate secretarial cover for such periods. The more notice you can give the better, from all parties' points of view, of work which will involve unsocial hours. Explain that you have business requirements which mean that the job must be progressed over the weekend. Most professionals will accept this where such reasons exist.

Be prepared for a higher charge at such times and ask the professional for details of any overtime charges which you will have to pay. The hourly charging rates may increase for such periods worked out of office hours. You are also likely to be billed for secretarial overtime.

Rule 5
Doing a deal quickly can save money

A matter should not be undertaken so quickly that all the issues are not properly thought out, but imposing a tight timetable focuses everyone's minds wonderfully and ensures that the work is done efficiently. There is no chance of increasing time costs by spending too long on a matter when the deal must be done quickly.

HOURLY CHARGING RATES

Some firms will tell you that they do not have hourly charging rates, but most do. As explained above, assisting the professional in minimising the time spent on a matter should help to reduce the cost. The rates themselves will be open to negotiation. Many companies, when first instructing a firm, will agree percentage off the rates, say 10 per cent. If you then require that bills be sufficiently detailed to give the number of hours worked by each fee earner and the cost of those hours, you can keep a check on that for which you have been billed.

The letter of engagement from the professional may make it clear that rates may increase from time to time. Agree fixed rates for an initial period, perhaps twelve months, and enter in your diary the necessity for an annual negotiation over what the following year's rates might be.

Many companies have no idea what sort of rates are reasonable. Going to a number of different firms for estimates originally will assist in making a fair comparison and give you an idea of the levels prevalent in your area. Professional bodies themselves do not set rates for work undertaken by their members. You will only find out the hourly charging rates by asking the individual firms.

In central London, for specialist legal advice, expect to pay £100–£300 per hour, depending on whether a partner or a more junior assistant is undertaking the work. Elsewhere rates may be as 'low' as half that sum. The difference is almost entirely caused by higher overheads and specialisation. Office rental costs and salaries are markedly higher in London. The more specialised firms are usually concentrated in the City.

Rates for accountants and other professionals may not differ much. With surveyors and architects, you are more likely to be quoted the cost of undertaking the work, such as a survey fee or the charges for designing and planning a building.

Consultants will often quote a daily rate. Ensure that you are aware of how many hours are covered in their typical day, so that a proper comparison can be made.

Most firms now quote a charging rate rather than a 'cost rate'; ensure that you are aware which rate has been quoted to you. A cost rate simply comprises the cost of the work undertaken by a particular individual within the firm, such that if that rate were earned, then all the costs of the transaction, including salaries and a proportion of overheads, would be covered. This would not be the rate you would pay, as the firm would also expect to make a profit. You really need to know the charging rate. If the firm does not disclose or calculate such a rate, then at least obtain an estimate or go to a firm which will quote its charging rates to you.

OTHER FACTORS

Time is one important factor in many professional bills. It is not the only factor and indeed professional rules often require that account be taken of a number of factors, including the value of the transaction. If the professional plans to charge a fee based on a percentage of the value of a transaction, referred to above, then find out from him what the level is and also discuss whether it is appropriate to have a fee fixed on that basis for that transaction. If you suspect that this will result in a higher bill than straight time charges, then suggest that a percentage charge is not a fair method of settling the fees. However, at least there is certainty with such a charge. Consultants, for example, asked to fix a rate, will estimate how long they expect the job to take and then add on a margin, in case of error, before quoting a rate to you. You may prefer to pay this margin (which could be more than you would otherwise have paid with straight time charging) rather than risk that a project will overrun.

Fees may also reflect the importance of the matter and its complexity, and whether the work involved unsocial hours or overtime.

Extra charges

Your professional's bill will also be subject to value added tax and 'disbursements'. For example, a solicitor may pay stamp duty and Land Registry fees on your behalf on a property transaction or the fees of any barristers instructed. Your patent agent will pay registration and renewal fees and the cost of instructing foreign agents. All these items will be added to your bill.

Ask your professional what additional charges may be included on bills if he does not deal with the issue in the letter of engagement. You should ask:

- Do you pay for photocopying undertaken in carrying out your work and, if so, at what rate?
- Do you pay for telephone charges? Some firms have systems which record on computer all calls above a certain value, which are then charged to the client.
- Do you pay for secretarial overtime or even general secretarial services? Some firms are moving towards time charging for secretaries too, rather than absorbing such cost into the general overhead figure in the charge-out rates.
- Are there any other costs you will be required to pay, such as the direct costs of facsimile transmissions?

BILLING METHODS

A good way of keeping costs under control is to require that a bill be sent to you at least monthly and possibly even fortnightly. Monthly billing is helpful for most companies and you would be billed even for matters which were still ongoing on an interim basis. Monthly billing enables you to ascertain the level to which costs have risen. Ensuring that you promptly pay the bills when due will keep your relationship with your professional sweet.

Many firms listen favourably to novel suggestions for charging. These include:

- retainers;
- success fees;
- itemised bills;
- fixed fees;
- caps.

Consider whether you would like to operate using any of them.

Retainers

A fixed sum to be paid monthly for all minor matters can help you keep costs down and means that you feel less anxious about telephoning the professional for occasional advice, as it will be covered in the retainer. The professional will not agree a retainer without a cap and it should be set out in writing what is and what is not covered by the retainer. Larger matters may result in a separate file being opened, with smaller matters or occasional telephone advice covered by the retainer, unless the amount of time which is incurred in satisfying the retainer begins to exceed a level agreed.

Consider how often you consult your professional over each quarter and the likely cost. Then suggest to him that you guarantee to pay that sum regularly. He has the certainty of income from you and you know what the charges will be.

Retainers of this sort are not the ultimate panacea. Both parties need to ensure that they do not exploit the relationship, by making too much use of the professional's time ostensibly under the retainer or, on his part, by doing little in return for it because he is assured of the money anyway. However, they can be useful. To assist in their success, provide that there will be regular reviews of how the retainer is operating and agree to alter its terms if circumstances change. They are a good way of keeping in regular touch with a professional without being too concerned about what it will cost.

Ask your professional if he would consider offering a form of telephone hotline service, as a variation on a retainer. You might telephone for no more than 5–10 minutes at a time for a fixed annual fee.

Retainers are used by many types of professionals, including solicitors and management consultants. A small company might pay a few thousand pounds a year to be able to call the consultant with queries up to a fixed number of hours over the year, and also have the benefit of a site visit from the consultant for a fixed number of days a year.

Success fees

You might like to agree that a lower charge will be payable if a transaction does not end successfully. There is nothing more depressing than paying a large solicitor's bill for time spent on an abortive acquisition. However, the professional has spent as much time and effort on a transaction whether or not it goes ahead, so he will certainly be entitled to be paid.

You might like to agree at the outset that if the transaction does not proceed to fruition then there will a reduction on the time charged, say 10–20 per cent, but that if the matter proceeds then a mark-up of a certain percentage over the time costs can be charged, or a charge based on the value of the transaction, which may not be as easy to justify in the event that a deal falls through.

In the USA contingency fees are permitted and are common for certain types of transactions. The professional does not get paid at all, or only a small amount, in the event of failure, but if a case is successful then the attorney can keep a percentage of the sum recovered in litigation from the other party. Such a method of charging is not yet common in this country and is not allowed by all professional bodies.

In the UK the situation is not as liberal. In 1993 the Government was considering preparing an order under section 58 of the Courts and Legal Services Act, allowing lawyers to make conditional fee arrangements with their clients in personal injury and insolvency cases, as well as cases before the European Court of Human Rights. A maximum uplift permitted was proposed at various figures from 20 to 100 per cent. The position on this and other novel billing arrangements under the various professional rules is fast-moving, with a general trend towards liberalisation. In practice, the answer is to ask for such arrangements. If they are forbidden, your professional adviser will soon tell you.

Some consultancy bodies, such as the Management Consultancies Association, forbid their members to charge by results, as the outcome could be short-term solutions, to the detriment of a better, longer-term solution. However, not all consultants are members of such associations and it may be appropriate to pay a consultant on the results or cost savings which are achieved. This method has much to recommend it in those areas where it is possible to judge the result and therefore is particularly useful for certain types of consultancy work, such as the implementation of new systems within a company.

Itemised bills

Ask that bills specify the amount of time that has been spent by each professional who has worked on a matter, with a brief description of what that person has done. This concentrates the mind of the professional wonderfully as to whether a piece of work undertaken can really be charged for and can result in lower bills. If you are not happy with the explanation of what someone has done on your file, then ask for further details.

It is more effort for the professional to have such a detailed bill drawn up, but you should always seek to negotiate this facility where possible. Suggest that your professional opens a separate file within his system each time you instruct him on a new piece of work. This ensures that you do not receive a bill on a 'general' file, where it is difficult to see what work has been done. The itemised bill should, of course, show all the individual disbursements which the professional has incurred. Require that the professional informs you before incurring disbursements above a certain fixed figure, say £100.

You would expect to see on the itemised bill details of the individuals who have worked on the matter and the amount of time which they have spent, in addition to a description of the work which they have done. Some professionals' bills are extremely unhelpful and do not set out with any clarity work which has been undertaken. This can be the fault of the firm, in having its costs department draw up the narrative for the bill, when it is the professional who has done the work who is best able to describe the work which has been undertaken. Always check the figures on the bill to ensure that the total has been correctly calculated, as errors are found from time to time.

Also, read carefully the rates which appear on the bill for the individuals. You may have thought you had negotiated a special discount on the charging rates, but this does not appear on the bill. Also, you may have agreed that fees would be frozen for a year and yet a recent increase in charging rates generally has been passed on to you, perhaps because the individual preparing the bill was not aware of the freeze which had been agreed.

It is up to you to check the bill and ensure that it is returned for correction. Having a detailed, itemised bill enables such a check to be carried out properly. A bill which just states a short description of work done and a final figure cannot be checked in this way.

Does the number of hours which appears on the bill correspond to the amount of work which you thought was being undertaken on your behalf? A firm may be screwed down by you to a very low charging rate and then simply make a profit by inflating the hours; not honest, of course, but it is very hard for you to check how much time has been spent. If you have an initial estimate, that makes it harder for such practices to be adopted.

An itemised bill will not usually state how much time was spent doing every single part of a job, such as 'writing a letter on 15th March, one hour'. If you are not happy with your itemised bill, then ask for a detailed breakdown of this sort. The professional may be reluctant to do so, because of the time and effort involved, but if this will result in the firm being paid, such a breakdown is likely to be forthcoming.

> **The important point to note in relation to itemised bills is that they should show all the information which you require.**

Some professionals' ideas as to what comprises an itemised bill do not tally with what is expected by the client. Some major companies issue instructions to their professional advisers around the world setting out the minimum standards and 'rules' to which they expect adherence in relation to billing. These typically state what information must appear on the itemised bill generally required by such systems.

Fixed fees

Whether you can agree a fixed fee for work to be done will depend on how keen the professional is to do your work. It means that he is taking the risk that a transaction will not cost him more than you agree. If he is confident in his prediction of how long the work will take, then a fixed fee may be possible. The difference between the fixed fee and the estimate considered above is that the fixed fee is just that — fixed, even if it subsequently transpires that there is a lot more work involved than was originally anticipated.

Always try to agree a fixed fee if you can. It must be said that accountants and solicitors are loath to accept charging on such a basis, so you may not be successful. However, some such deals have been negotiated and an efficient and careful firm can even ensure that it makes a good profit from fixed fee work. The fixed fee may appear more expensive as a firm will allow for a margin of error in setting the fee, but you will have the certainty that the job will cost what you expect and can budget accordingly.

Caps

Agreeing that in no event will fees exceed a certain level will be a stronger means of keeping fees down than a general, nonbinding estimate. Again, it will be a matter for negotiation between the parties as to what they agree on having a cap. It is always worth trying to negotiate such a ceiling.

You may be able to combine an estimate with an overall cap. Many companies are able to negotiate such arrangements with their professional advisers.

OBTAINING THE BEST DEAL

The best deal for you may not be the cheapest. You will be looking for quickness of response and quality of advice, as well as value for money. However, the cost of the service is not irrelevant and it is certainly always worth discussing costs and the basis upon which fees will be levied. If you are unhappy about a bill rendered, then say so. A telephone call may provoke a better response than a formal letter of complaint. Be firm and suggest a reduction in a bill if you are not happy with its level and believe that your concerns are justified.

It is no good agreeing a beneficial charging regime if you do not keep a check on the professional's bills. Have one individual responsible within your company for checking professional bills received, and arrange to review regularly how the deal you have negotiated with your professional has operated in practice.

Most professional bodies (listed in Appendix 2) have procedures that you can follow if you wish to take the matter further than the firm to whose charges you object. Costs can be taxed, or a remuneration certificate obtained, from the Law Society for solicitors' costs in appropriate circumstances. Complain first to the firm. You may have been given details of the internal complaints procedure in the letter of engagement. The individual partner who did the work should be your first port of call, followed by the senior partner.

Many who query their professional fees find that they can reach some compromise and a reduction in the bill, if that is fair and the complaint is justified. If you query all bills on principle, you are less likely to be accommodated and issued with a reduced bill.

There may be circumstances in which it is fair to share the bill with another company or business. If there is any such arrangement, then let the professional know at the outset. He will need to discover whether he is allowed to act for you and the other company. He will not be able to do so when there is a conflict of interest between the two parties involved; when they are both on the same 'side', it may be possible. It should be clarified at the outset who will be legally responsible for paying the bill.

Areas in which there can be some confusion are where there is an individual proprietor of a company and it is not clear whether the company or the owner is the client, or where a joint venture is set up. The interests of the joint venture company may not be the same as either one of its parent companies.

Be clear and fair. Ensure that the professional knows that costs are important to you. That alone may result in his being careful to undertake work for you efficiently. Always be upfront about money. The professional is in business, as much as you are, to make a profit.

XYZ Co has just recruited a new employee whose brief is to cut professional charges. Jill Saveit's salary is linked to savings which she makes on the annual professional charges which XYZ Co pays. She begins by examining all the records of the relationship with the professional advisers used by XYZ.

In many cases firms had been used for years and it was not clear why such firms had been chosen, nor was there anything in writing setting out the terms of business between the companies. In one instance there was a disagreement over a bill, which the firm agreed to reduce, but generally a variety of advisers had been used, without any coherent plan.

Jill examines the most recent bills rendered by the professional firms used by XYZ. One firm, in particular, seems to have steeply increased its charges in recent years, but this is not very clear as the charge-out rates are not apparent from the file.

Jill calls into her office those individuals within the firm who most frequently instruct the professionals. Again there appears to be no coherent system as to who has authority to instruct outside advisers. Some parts of the business frequently use outside advisers, where others do not. Some use different firms from others. Staff explain that they have had no guidance on whom they should use and have simply used either firms which the company has used for years, or firms with whom they had connections, or an earlier relationship when they worked elsewhere.

Jill determines to rationalise the system. She begins by drawing up lists of the different firms which the company is already using. She draws up lists, including other firms of which she is aware, having undertaken some research on the types of firms which are required. The company has a large number of staff and has been involved in some rather nasty employment disputes. A personnel consultant could usefully be added to the list of professionals and the firm which has handled the employment law queries of XYZ has not been responding particularly quickly to requests for advice.

Armed with her short-lists, Jill consults those within the firm who are involved with professional advisers and begins a consultation process, which extends to board level.

The next stage is to contact those firms which are on the short-lists for different types of professional advice and arrange for them to send some relevant material. Two do not respond at all. Jill crosses them off the list. Appointments are arranged to meet the others. Jill prepares a list of questions to which she requires answers at the meetings and sends these beforehand, so that the firms concerned have the chance to put their views. She asks about the way the firms are structured and their experience, as well as questions about billing.

She also encloses a summary of the billing and other arrangements which she would like to see in place with the professional firms. This includes a requirement for monthly itemised billing and goes into detail such as that professional advisers should book air tickets through XYZ, that photocopying should be included in the charge-out rates, that rates are fixed for twelve months and will only rise after negotiation, if agreed.

Jill also prepares an internal document which requires that no professional adviser can be instructed with a new matter unless via Jill. She proposes that she is the point of contact. This produces uproar within XYZ. Jill listens to the points made and accommodates the concerns expressed by appointing two other individuals within the firm who can also arrange professional appointments when Jill is not available. She also changes the draft proposal so that she does not pass on the instructions to the advisers, but gives consent in advance before the instruction goes ahead. She, therefore, is able to be involved in billing and negotiation of rates, but is not in the position of having to explain at second hand facts on which she is not fully briefed.

Following meetings with the potential advisers, Jill, in conjunction with other members of staff present at the presentations or beauty parades, decides which firms to instruct. In one case they remain with the firm they already use, but renegotiate their billing arrangements. They decide for one discipline to have two firms competing with each other and in all other cases have one new set of advisers.

The system is reviewed every year and has resulted in substantial savings on professional bills. There is now much less duplication of effort. Jill receives copies of all professional opinions received so that she will check in advance before work is put out whether there is already the expertise or an earlier opinion which the company holds.

Keeping a close watch on your professional costs and adopting some of the methods of reducing costs described in this chapter should result in substantial savings on professional bills.

CHECKLIST

- Recognise that all professional fees are potentially negotiable

- Do not be embarrassed about raising the issue of fees. Do not assume that the professional will mention the subject first

- Consider regional firms instead of London practices with higher overheads

- Mention fees early on and always get a specific written estimate

- Help the professional to keep costs down by undertaking as much mundane work for him as is feasible. Minimise the time which the professional spends on the matter, as time is the most important factor in most professional bills

- Remain in the driving seat. You are the client. You pay the bill. Act assertively in questioning if two professionals are needed at a meeting or whether first-class travel is necessary, etc.

- Consider the novel billing methods described in this chapter: retainers, success fees, itemised bills, fixed fees and caps. Check bills as they arrive and renogotiate rates each year

5
Maintaining a good relationship

A professional is a person expert in some field of activity who shares the responsibility for decisions, and gives a service to others in that part of their affairs to which the professional's expertise applies, bringing to bear in this participation wider values than those he is advising may necessarily themselves consider relevant.

G W Higgin, 1964

The relationship between professional and client comprises considerably more than the client trying to pay as little as he can get away with and the professional trying to squeeze as much money as possible out of the client. In this chapter the factors which contribute to making a relationship between professional and client successful and rewarding for both parties will be examined.

Working well with your professional will ensure that effective use is made of both parties' respective abilities. Learning how you can help the professional is the first step in your maintaining a good relationship with him or her.

COMMUNICATION

Communication is the key to most successful relationships, whether business or personal. The majority of misunderstandings arise through a breakdown in communication. You cannot read the professional's mind, nor can you expect him to be able to read yours. Make it clear what you want done and expect him to explain to you what he has undertaken on your behalf.

If you wish to maintain an ongoing relationship with a professional, then keep in touch between transactions. Some firms are good at keeping in touch with clients, whether by production of a newsletter, taking you out to lunch or organising client seminars, or by simply telephoning you from time to time to see how things are. Clearly you do not want to be forever pestering your professional with pointless telephone calls, but if there are important developments within your company or firm, why not write to your usual professional advisers and tell them about the changes? They will often find out only from reading the newspapers what is going on. If you let them know in advance of proposed changes or large contracts being won, they may even be able to offer you some helpful advice.

Similarly, you should expect your professional adviser to keep you informed about major changes in his practice and, more importantly, how the matter upon which he is advising you is developing. If you have not heard for some time, then telephone him and ask for regular progress reports. It could be that he is very busy on other matters and is secretly thankful that your matter has become inactive. A discreet call from you might spur him into action.

Matters which appear to go dead usually suffer from not having one individual in the driving-seat, keen to take the matter forward. There is no reason why you should not assume that role yourself, calling your opposite number (though you should not telephone the other party's solicitor or other adviser if they are using professional advisers themselves). A meeting between business clients can often push a matter forward and assist your professional adviser in progressing a matter.

Ask your adviser what input he requires from you and supply whatever he requires as promptly as possible. If you are able, send material by fax. This makes it appear more urgent, even if it is not, and can spur the adviser into doing something about the matter. Telephone the adviser before you send the fax, telling him it is coming, explaining what it is about and making him personally interested and involved in the matter. Receiving a letter or fax with no personal contact imposes less of a feeling of moral obligation to act promptly than if a one-to-one conversation is held. Now, this is not to suggest that you necessarily need to resort to tricks to persuade a professional to undertake any work for you. However, any method which will ensure that your matter, over other companies', is given greater prominence is ultimately bound to help you in having the matter looked at more promptly.

If you simply send a letter and it is not acknowledged within a day or two, telephone the firm and find out who is handling the matter. This will not always be the individual to whom you wrote. What can happen is that a letter is received by one individual, who is desperately busy. Intending to handle the matter personally he lets it sit on his desk whilst other, even more pressing matters are handled. Finally, guiltily, he hands it to a colleague, who will then need several further days to consider the matter. Better if the first individual receives a telephone call from you, explains, during the telehone conversation, that he is busy and immediately passes the work on.

You should not be apologetic about your requirements or denigrate the matter which you require handling by the professional. Set clear deadlines and telephone if they are not met.

Imagine the following scenario, which illustrates the breakdown in relationships between professionals and their clients. Company K manufactures a product which it wishes to begin exporting to continental Europe. It writes a letter to its solicitor along the following lines:

Dear Mr. Smith,

We intend to begin exporting our products to France and then throughout Europe shortly. Please advise us of our legal obligations.

Yours sincerely,

The solicitor responds by describing in great detail (at Company

K's expense) all the methods of exporting to Europe, the reams of EC regulations which might be applicable and how they should be accommodated.

Company K's managing director, being a very busy person, puts the letter in a drawer meaning to look at it in due course. Subsequently a rather large bill appears, which is reluctantly paid by the MD, who is still feeling guilty that he has not considered the advice received. Exports to France have begun without any thought as to the legal implications and the company may subsequently infringe some rule or regulation, details of which were hidden in the long letter.

What should Company K have done? First, the letter to the solicitor was far too brief. An extreme example has been used here. In practice, few individuals would write such a non-specific letter to their adviser, though many letters to advisers are confusing and lacking in essential information. If you are not a great letter writer and feel intimidated by the thought of writing a letter to a solicitor or other professional adviser, write a short letter and discuss the matter over the telephone.

In general it is preferable that as much as possible is reduced to writing. You will then have the opportunity later, simply by looking up your letter on the file, to see what advice you requested and what was given in response, but bear in mind that the production of a letter is much more expensive than a telephone conversation. The professional will have to think about the letter, probably check the position more carefully before writing about the matter, and finally will need to prepare the letter, check it and dispatch it. More time, more money and not always a better response.

Had you begun by discussing the matter over the telephone with the professional, then you could have clarified what advice you required and not had a response which covered all sorts of areas, only some of which were relevant to you.

In every case it is useful to consider, before instructing the professional, what type of response you require. At times urgency will mean that only an oral response will be possible, but where there is an option consider whether the advice required wil be referred to again and whether you will need to disseminate it to other people within your organisation. If you will, it will be best to ask for written advice, rather than attempt to summarise the advice yourself for the benefit of your colleages. If you know that you will be required to produce a summary in any event, because you could never present the colleagues with the type of voluminous advice you generally receive from those advisers, then tell the advisers of the problem and require that they produce advice which is easy to read and clear as to its recommendations.

Returning to the example, the client could have improved the chance of receiving the advice he required by telephoning and discussing the matter first. He could have explained:

1. The nature of the products to be exported;
2. how he proposed to enter the market, whether he would appoint an exclusive distributor or agent or whatever;
3. what types of exporting issues he was concerned about; whether he had read some articles about health and safety laws or whether he was concerned about product liability.

The professional, in this hypothetical example, should have called the client with further questions, before running up costs on what could inevitably lead to advice requiring the client to find the proverbial needle in the haystack. Alternatively, the professional should have sent a short letter asking for further information, or warning the client that a large range of issues would need to be addressed. It could be that the client had not yet decided, for example, whether he would exploit the EC market by selling his goods through an agent on commission, or a distributor who would take the risk and resell the goods at his own profit, or even whether the client would be prepared to grant a licence of his manufacturing technology so that a European company could manufacture the products itself and sell them abroad under a royalty-bearing licence.

The pro-active professional would ensure that all options were raised and their respective advantages and disadvantages discussed with the client, unless the client had already decided on the best method of export for him.

Not communicating enough information is not the only

communication problem which can arise. Sometimes either party will communicate inaccurately. The client may fire off a letter to the accountant without thinking through all the issues. It is no good taking the attitude that the professional is there to deal with all the issues in one particular area and that the client does not need to consider the matter at all. Often, it is only the client who has sufficient inside information to enable the professional to deal with a matter adequately. Your time may be valuable and you may be very short of time, particularly time spent on what does not look like cash-earning activities, like briefing professional advisers. However, spending time thoroughly briefing advisers is time well spent and should lead to reduced bills in the end and better advice obtained from the adviser. Giving the adviser the full facts, rather than the potted version you might produce if you cannot be bothered to go through your files, will reduce the risk of a failure of communication between the parties.

Time and again in practice, clients present a clouded picture of the situation upon which they want advice. Often the 'iceberg' scenario arises. The client highlights one problem and a few weeks later, after the professional has begun working on the matter, it transpires — through looking at the papers which have been sent to the professional, or by information received from other parties to a transaction or legal action — that there are many other areas which are relevant, but which the client did not see fit to mention at the outset.

Be totally honest with the professional.

It does not pay to lie to those on your side. The adviser will find it hard to advise you properly if you hide facts from him or paint an inaccurate picture.

This works both ways. Professionals rarely have cause to lie to clients, unless there is negligence or fraud on the part of the professional (to be considered later). However, advice from professionals can be too long. Do not be afraid of telling the adviser that you are only interested in a short letter of advice. A longer letter may appear to justify a bigger bill on the professional's part, but in fact it need not. Writing a short letter containing all the salient facts may take longer and be a better piece of professional advice than a letter from someone who is able to spew out many, often irrelevant references to regulations or statutes, or whatever.

This is not to say that you will never have the opposite problem, of an adviser not spending sufficient time on your matter, perhaps because he is busy with other work, resulting in your receiving skimpy advice which is clearly not appropriate. If you require a more thorough job, say so, tactfully.

GETTING ON WELL

Ensuring that you get on well with your professional advisers is not only a question of communicating what your requirements are, but also a matter of basic psychology. You do not have to like each other, although that obviously helps, but getting along implies the usual give and take. You should not be kow-towing to the professional, but expecting a quality efficient service. Each party should hold respect for the other.

Over the years you may become friends. You may go out to lunch together from time to time, exchange pleasantries and discuss matters of mutual interest. Invite the professional over to your factory or workshop or other premises. It can assist him greatly to be able to visualise your products and have some idea of your business and how it is organised. This should help in maintaining a good relationship between you and the adviser.

Some professionals, particularly management consultants, may be based at your offices for significant periods of time. This brings its own problems and also opportunities. There is much greater scope for the consultant to get to know your company really well and the people within it. You are also more likely to be around to answer questions and your instructions to the consultant have a greater chance of being clear and comprehensive than instructions imparted to a professional adviser often located miles away, over a short telephone call. Alas, not every company and consultant is able to exploit the advantages of working in close proximity in this way. You may be too busy to give the proper attention necessary to the consultant.

If you know that will be the case, consider appointing someone else as the liaison point and ensure that the chosen individual is properly briefed.

As discussed in Chapter 3, you should have made it clear, preferably in a written contract with the consultant, where he is to be located and who pays for what. You may have agreed to provide him with secretarial services at your premises. If you did not establish this at the beginning of the relationship and you are not happy with what the consultant has assumed you wil provide, then tell him so. It can be advantageous to meet regularly, even if there is very little to say. Such meetings can be brief, but will give each of you the opportunity to raise any concerns and give you a chance to check that the consultant is getting on with the job in the way that you require.

Solutions, not problems

The best professional relationships arise where the professional does more than answer the question put to him. He should be a business facilitator. You want from him solutions and not problems. If his letters to you are too voluminous or unclear, do not assume there is something wrong with you. It is easy in any business to produce a letter full of jargon not intelligible to the layman. The competent professional will have, over the years, honed his skill in distilling the important facts and presenting them in a manner understandable to the individual to whom the letter is addressed.

Again, communication is at issue here. Tell him that you want shorter letters and telephone him to discuss the matters which you do not understand. You are not paying hundreds of pounds to take advice which you cannot understand, never mind put into practice.

Ask what the problem is and what solutions there are to it. You want his advice presented in a positive way. If you cannot undertake a job in the way you wish, what other ways are possible? If the building cannot be rebuilt so as to include the meeting rooms where you expected, you want to know how the problem could be overcome or where else they could be situated. Your adviser should ideally give you suggestions, too, as to how to run your business better. There may be changes in law or accounting practice which are of interest or use to you. The professional who is a successful business facilitator will pass on such relevant information to you and show you what use you can make of it. He can draw on his experience with other companies and firms and offer advice of a general business nature, where appropriate.

If you really just want him to fulfil a discrete advisory role and you resent his other efforts, which you regard as him trying to tell you how to run your business, then tell him so, politely. However, most companies welcome a pro-active adviser who takes on more of a role of counsellor.

The adviser probably has a range of contacts amongst other professionals. He may have access to venture capital companies or contacts with merchant banks, with whom he could put you in touch. Make full use of those of his resources which are available and you will be better served.

Changing faces

People leave, both within your company and at your professional's practice. This can jeopardise long-nourished relationships. Being a professional adviser is a very personal role. You, the client, pay a firm's bills, but you may only use one individual within a firm. In fact, only using one person can be a bad idea. It is dangerous to depend on one adviser, who will inevitably be away on holiday and involved on other matters from time to time. It is much better to develop relationships with a number of people who specialise in the area in which you require advice. In that way you will not feel so exposed when your professional leaves to join another practice. If you prefer him to any other then there is absolutely no reason why you should not move firms with the professional. You will need to ensure that all outstanding bills with the old practice are paid and that they are aware of the change.

When a new employee within your company replaces the individual with whom the professional has always dealt to date then ensure a smooth handover and full briefing sessions, so that the new person is aware of what work was outstanding when his colleague left and how it can be taken forward. New people may have their own contacts amongst professionals. It will simply be a matter of how you stipulate within your company which professionals are used as to whether or not the new employee will be allowed to transfer to his preferred firm. Keeping relationships amicable, even when a professonal relationship is being severed, is important. You never know when in the future you may wish to use that professional firm again.

PAYING BILLS

Money: you are not going to be the best regarded client if you always pay your bills late or not at all, or always query the level of the bill.

> **Establish what payment period you and the adviser regard as reasonable and stick to it.**

If you have trouble in meeting bills for professionals then consider some of the alternative charging methods mentioned in the previous chapter, particularly arranging for bills to be sent more frequently and, thus, for smaller amounts.

> Company U receives a huge accountancy bill, with virtually no descriptive narrative describing what work was done. The company secretary to whom the bill was addressed is outraged, but becomes distracted with other matters. He puts the bill away in his pending drawer and leaves it there. Six weeks later he receives a gentle reminder from the accountancy firm, which he ignores. Sterner letters follow, finally sent to the chairman of the board, who went to school with the senior partner of the accountancy firm. The company secretary is instructed to pay the bill at once and does so. He is made to feel in the wrong.

It would have been much better if, on receiving the bill, the company secretary had looked at it within a matter of days, checked it was accurate and asked for a fuller description. If satisfied, the bill should have been paid within 30 days or whatever period had been agreed. The period may have been stipulated in intial correspondence or a letter of engagement between the accountant and the client. Where a fuller description was requested, when it arrived it should have been considered and if the company secretary still thought the figure unjustifiable, he should either have tackled the partner who was responsible for the bill at the acccountancy practice over the telephone, or put the complaint in writing, in the hope that some settlement could be reached. Many professional bills are disputed and compromises (ie reductions in figures) are agreed every day. Not all clients are aware of this.

If you are having trouble paying, perhaps because of cashflow problems, it may be better to agree stage payments of a bill, rather than pay nothing and find that the firm soon refuses to undertake any further work for you. Traditionally, professional advisers have not been very good at running their own businesses and have been too 'gentlemanly' to have good credit control. They have learnt this to their cost in the difficult economic climate of today. If you recognise a reluctance on the part of your professional adviser to tackle you over payment of a bill, do not exploit his weakness. It is unlikely to earn you any favours when you next require an urgent piece of work to be done.

Indeed, barristers whose fees are paid by solicitors are not allowed to sue for non-payment of fees. Other professionals have no such constraints and are even able in some cases to exercise what is known as a 'lien' (ie the right to retain possession until the relevant debt is discharged) over files which they hold in relation to your business. This effectively means that they can hold on to your files and refuse to send them to the client or any new firm of professional advisers whom you may appoint.

Good professional and client relationships are not created from such difficulties. However, when you have a genuine grievance over a bill or the way that a matter has been handled, then the withholding of payment is the best method of ensuring that a compromise is reached. As in any other business, it is hard to induce a refund after a bill has been paid, but a professional concerned about cashflow may prefer something rather than the hope of full payment later.

EXAMINING BILLS

When you receive a bill for professional fees examine it closely. Take the following steps, although not all professionals will draw up their bills in the same way or reveal the same information on bills. You have already been advised to require your professional to send you an itemised bill (see Chapter 4).

Addressee

Does the bill correctly name your firm? Some clients do not adequately brief their professional about the company within their group to which bills should be sent. You may have accounting problems if the invoice is issued to the wrong company. Send the bill back to be changed if the incorrect company name is shown.

A related issue is where a bill is sent to one part of an organisation and where different items of work are shown on the bill, so that you can then allocate the bill between parts of the group. Ask for separate bills, instead. Often there will be a centralised system for briefing professionals within large groups of companies. It can be easier to despatch bills to the relevant parts of the organisation which requested the work, where either separate bills are prepared for separate matters or it is clear from the bill how much of the sums due relate to the separate matters shown thereon. Alternatively, you may have a very informal group structure where it does not matter at all to whom a bill is addressed, so this may not be an important issue for you.

Also check that the bill has been sent to the right address and individual. The professional should be told to whom bills should be addressed. It is preferable if bills are sent to an individual within the organisation who is familiar with the work which has been done, rather than just to the accounts department, which will not have any idea whether charges are justified or not. For larger groups, one individual may be keeping a check on professional fees and that person could receive all bills for professional fees and then copy them for comment to the individuals or departments for whom the work was done. Finally, when the bill is approved for payment, it can be sent to the accounts department. If your company operates a corporate policy of paying bills particularly slowly, it can assist in maintaining a friendly relationship with your professional advisers if you give the accounts department instructions to override the general rule of late payment for professional bills which have been approved by you.

Period covered by the bill

Check that the period covered by the bill appears on the bill and that you have not been billed for this period before. It helps to compare the latest bill with the one before for this purpose and to make a comparison of the level of fees charged. If you have asked for monthly billing to keep costs down, check that this has been done. Also, look at the date on the bill. If it is a recent bill but relates to work undertaken some time ago, then you may like to enquire about what the current level of costs is, so that you have some idea of what size the next bill will be.

The arithmetic

It is not unheard of for professional bills, even from accountants, not to add up correctly. Get a calculator out and check the figures, including the VAT.

The description of work done

Consider carefully the narrative on the bill which describes what the professional has done. Is it what you asked him to do? Does it include work you issued no instructions for? Is the description full enough for you to determine whether the bill is justified or not? If not, then ask for further details. It can be helpful to ask for details concerning the work done by particular individuals, so that you can ascertain whether there has been any overmanning or effective double charging.

The charges

Look at the figure for costs. Is it reasonable? Take the trouble to get out your file and check if an estimate was given by the firm for the cost of the work. If it was, and it has not been adhered to, then insist that it is or at least that an explanation satisfactory to you is offered as to why there has been a departure from the figures given originally. Does the bill show the charging rates of the individuals undertaking your work?

If the professional is the sort who charges principally by the time spent on a matter, the firm will have time records, usually stored on computer, and easily ought to be able to prepare a bill which sets out, for example, 'Mrs K, 16 hours at £105 per hour', for each of the individuals who worked on the matter. Such bills are commonly prepared in this fashion, though not all clients are aware that this facility is available. When this information appears on the bill you will be able to see just how long has been spent on a matter. It may be far too long and you may be able to negotiate a reduction on that basis. Also, it will enable an examination of the charging rates to be made. Check if you agreed, when originally instructing the firm, that lower rates would apply or that you would be granted a percentage discount from their normal charging rates. Complain if the firm has got that wrong. If they argue that their rates have increased since you last agreed rates, check whether or not you agreed a freeze on rates for a particular period.

It can do no harm to talk with other clients (if you know them) to find out what they are paying. You may be able to negotiate a reduction on the basis of what others are paying, though many companies will wish to keep that information confidential and the firm is unlikely to release it. Firms may have what appears to be a very high hourly charging rate, but then, in practice, rarely agree the full rate with clients, most paying a lower sum negotiated from the higher rate.

Check that value added tax is not included where this is

unnecessary, for example, where the client billed operates outside the EC.

Disbursements

The bill is likely to include charges for various expenses which the professional has incurred on your behalf, such as taxi fares, flights or hotel bills. Check if the figures seem reasonable. You may have agreed that you would incur those charges directly, using discounts you may have negotiated with hotel groups, etc; alternatively, you may have agreed that the professional should travel economy class. The bill may be your only opportunity to check if this instruction has been carried out. Ask for further detail if the bill is not specific enough.

Other disbursements on a solicitor's bill would include barristers' fees or Land Registry Fees, stamp duty or foreign lawyers' fees. Patent agents would include renewal fees for patents or trademarks. Whatever the professional, check that the disbursements appear correct. Did you agree that telephone calls and photocopying would be separately charged for? Check.

Signature

Check that the bill has been signed.

The unscrupulous can delay payment of professionals fees for a considerable period of time by raising endless queries on the bill. This does not make for a harmonious professional relationship. Check bills carefully, but do this promptly and then pay them within the period agreed.

Check that your payment, when it is made, is acknowledged in writing.

GIFTS AND BRIBES

Should you give your professional adviser presents? The annual calendar, diary and bottle of the company whisky at Christmas is unlikely to damage the professional relationship and indeed is likely to buy you some cheap goodwill, particularly when you include all members of the team at the professional practice who have been assisting you throughout the year. Do not forget the adviser's secretary. Although in these days of well-equipped professional practices, with PCs on the desks of professionals and few professionals having the services of a secretary for their sole use, the power of the secretary is often diminished, it does no harm to maintain a good relationship with support staff as well as the professionals themselves. You may need a document urgently, which can only be produced if the secretary can be persuaded to cancel her plans for the evening.

More expensive presents to professionals are less likely to be well regarded and some firms may have rules forbidding the acceptance of larger gifts. Invitations to your annual general meeting and lunch are a good idea, and advisers with whom you are particularly pleased may appreciate an invitation to events at which you might have a box or suite, or other facilities for corporate entertaining. If you have a product which professionals might be interested in buying, you may like to offer selected advisers with whom you are especially pleased the opportunity to purchase the products at cost price or at a discount.

Never try to bribe a professional adviser.

CORPORATE INVOLVEMENT

Professional practices often forbid partners and employees to buy shares in clients' companies. This is very sensible. Be wary of a professional adviser who holds shares in your company. Indeed, it might be wise from time to time to make enquiries. Ask the partner who usually does your work to send a note around the firm to discover whether or not any of the partners or employees hold shares in your company. You may not have a problem if they do, but it is rarely sensible, unless you work for a huge listed company in which anyone with a reasonable portfolio of shares might be expected to hold shares. It is more in the interests of your professional advisers, rather than your company, that they do not hold shares in circumstances where they might be open to accusations of insider dealing. Never pass 'tips' to your advisers.

Some companies find it advantageous to invite a partner (sometimes a senior employee) of their professional advisers to sit on the Board of Directors. If you wish to do so, note that the adviser will expect to be paid in the usual way and make sure that you set out in writing the basis on which this much closer relationship will operate. You will need to define clearly when that individual is giving advice as a professional adviser and when as a director.

Many accountants and solicitors become company secretary to clients. For smaller firms, this removes the hassle of keeping statutory books up to date and remembering to submit Annual Returns, but it is not always cost-effective. The tasks involved are very mundane and will usually be delegated within the professional firm to a trainee. Companies of any size probably have sufficient manpower internally to take over this task themselves.

Where professional advisers are very closely involved in running a company, more so than simply by way of giving professional advice, they may become 'shadow directors', under the Companies Act 1985. Such individuals will be subject to a number of the duties which are placed on directors generally. Where professional advisers may be involved in the business to such an extent, always consider whether they are shadow directors in this way and seek advice as to the consequences.

Relationships may become so close with some advisers that you wish to recruit them. It is unlikely that there will be any non-solicitation clause in any contract with your professional advisers, principally because in many cases a short letter will be the only contract there is. However, this may not be the case, particularly with management consultants. Always look at the contract carefully and ensure that you reach a satisfactory compromise when you want to take on an employee in breach of a non-solicitation clause.

ONGOING RELATIONSHIPS

Many relationships with professionals last for years. They can be immensely satisfying and profitable. If you have a good relationship with a professional, make sure it stays that way. As soon as there is something with which you are not happy, then communicate that to the professional so that problems can be sorted out at an early stage rather than resolved by more drastic methods, the subject matter of the following chapter.

CHECKLIST

- Keep in touch with your professional advisers on a regular basis between transactions

- Telephone before writing to establish personal contact and fax rather than sending letters by post

- Give deadlines for receipt of advice, but do not describe everything as urgent as you will cease to be credible

- Brief professional advisers fully and send them all relevant information

- Ensure that you choose a professional adviser who is a business facilitator, rather than one who always raises reasons why a particular course of action cannot be undertaken, without suggesting alternative solutions

- Pay professionals within the payment period which you have agreed, if you want to be a popular client. Be careful in giving your advisers gifts; these should not overstep the boundary of legality and become bribes

- Consider if your advisers could have closer involvement with your company, perhaps by taking a seat on the Board or assuming the role of company secretary

6

Sacking the professional

A Profession may be defined simply as a trade which is organised, incompletely, no doubt, but genuinely, for the performance of the function. It is not simply a collection of individuals who get a living for themselves by the same kind of work. Nor is it merely a group which is organised exclusively for the economic protection of its members, though that is normally among its purposes. It is a body of men who carry on their work in accordance with rules designed to enforce certain standards both for the better protection of its members and for the better service of the public.

R H Tawney, 1921

This chapter has an emotive title. Can you really sack professionals? If they are not performing satisfactorily, then the easiest way to proceed may be to terminate your relationship, cancel the retainer between you, sever the client/professional relationship and proceed with another firm.

There are many other firms operating in this country who would welcome your business. No firm is indispensible and it is your right to choose and swap professionals when you so wish.

COMPLAINTS

There may simply be one aspect of the work which the professional has done for you with which you are not happy. You may not yet feel you wish to move your work to another practice. If this is the case, then make a complaint. As explained earlier, some professionals' rules of conduct require that members formulate a procedure for dealing with complaints and you may have been told about this in your letter of engagement.

Check you correspondence first to see what procedure has been set down. If there appears to be none, then first approach the person who has done the work for you. That is the fairest method of proceeding. There may be a legitimate reason or explanation for the way that the individual has handled the matter. There may be circumstances when you feel you should approach the partner in charge, the senior partner of the firm or even the relevant professional body (details of which appear in Appendix 2).

For example, if you think that your funds have been misappropriated or there is some other allegation of dishonesty or breach of confidentiality, then confronting the individual concerned will only tip him off. Fortunately, dishonesty by professionals is rare, but you should be aware that it does happen on occasion. You may be trusting your professional with large sums of money. Check on what basis money is held, document everything in writing and ensure you know whether, and on what basis, interest will be paid to you. Some professionals' rules of conduct specify the circumstances in which interest should be paid on client money.

There will be professional rules about the giving of undertakings by the professionals, ie formal promises that they will carry out what they have formally undertaken to do (this is the case with solicitors), the keeping of various types of account and indemnity insurance. Although you may well be able to recover money lost through dishonesty from the various professional body indemnity funds, it is clearly preferable to keep a close eye on matters to ensure that no theft of your money occurs in the first place. You may like to ensure that all money comes to you rather than having it held by the professional on your behalf, though this may not always be possible.

Generally, in the first instance you will address your complaint to the individual who is handling your matter. If you do not obtain a satisfactory answer, then take the matter up with the senior partner in the firm. Appendix 4 includes a draft letter of complaint, which would obviously have to be amended to suit the particular circumstance.

Expect a prompt answer. Solicitors, for example, are required to investigate complaints promptly (within 14 days, if possible) and thoroughly, and an explanation should be given to the client and appropriate action taken. If the client is still not happy, he should be informed by the solicitor that he can complain to the Solicitors Complaints Bureau (SCB, details in Appendix 2). The SCB publishes a leaflet, obtainable from them, entitled 'How and When', detailing the procedures for clients when contacting the SCB. Firms are recommended to give clients this leaflet when a client is still not happy, after having exhausted the internal complaints procedures of a firm.

You should expect your professional to investigate your complaint with seriousness and concern. An apology should be offered if appropriate and full explanations given.

Sometimes there is simply a personality clash between you and the professional. You may be entirely different types of people. If this is the case, take action before it is too late or more embarrassing. Express your concerns early on rather than have a major showdown later. The solution could be a simple exchange of staff, so that you deal with someone else at the professional's firm with whom you are able to get on better. Your complaint may be able to be resolved by a reduction in the costs which have been charged to you.

Complaining to a professional body

Most professional bodies have substantial powers to punish members who have not acted in accordance with their professional rules. Every week solicitors are struck off the Roll or suspended from practice. The Royal Institution of Chartered Surveyors has powers to reprimand, suspend or expel members for breach of professional rules or to require them to comply with undertakings to be given to the professional body. The Architects Registration Council of the United Kingdom has powers to terminate registration of those guilty of disgraceful conduct in their capacity as an architect. Other professional bodies have similar powers.

If you wish to make a complaint to a professional body, then write or telephone them first. Ask for their professional conduct or standards department. They will send you details of how to make a formal complaint. Check first that your professional is indeed a member of that professional body.

If there is a matter about which you are concerned, it is up to you to complain. In doing so you may well be protecting other companies from suffering at the hands of a dishonest or incompetent professional in the way that you have. How to sue a professional is considered in the next chapter.

SEVERING THE CONNECTION

There may be reasons why you prefer to move to another firm. There may be nothing wrong in terms of professional conduct with the firm which you have been using, but you have heard of another you would prefer to use, as they are cheaper or better regarded. How should you go about severing your connection?

There will be ongoing matters which it may not be sensible to transfer midstream. Indeed, many companies use several firms of professionals for different types of work. They may use a high-street legal practice for recovery of debts, a leading city firm for international takeovers, and a specialist niche practice for entertainment contracts.

You may go ahead and instruct a new firm on new matters and simply let the old continue until completion. It is wisest to tell the old firm what is happening; you do not want them to find out on the 'grapevine'. Keeping everything out in the open will ensure that any acrimony or resentment is minimised. Be prepared for firms which will try to persuade you to stay. Indeed, they may offer you such a better deal on costs that you will be persuaded to remain with them after all.

One issue that will have to be addressed is the handing over of files to the new firm. If you have not paid your bills at the first firm, then they may have a legal 'lien' or right of retention over your files and can rightfully refuse to send the files on to the new firm until the bill is paid. Make sure that you have a full summary prepared within your company, and ask for one from the first professional firm, of all bills outstanding and those which are yet to be rendered. Then make sure that payment is made as soon as possible and that the firm sends bills out for those matters which are waiting to be billed, so that you can get entirely up to date.

You do not have to offer an explanation as to why you are changing firms, but it will help to clear the air if you do. Tact and good humour should be used to the full. Offer thanks for work undertaken in the past and best wishes for the future, if you can bring yourself to do so. A letter formally terminating your relationship or 'retainer' should be sent by you. A specimen of such a letter is included in Appendix 4.

> A warning: if you are considering suing the previous firm, then always take legal advice before sending any correspondence, in case you prejudice your case later.

Ensure that you start off on a clear basis with the new firm and address problems as they arise.

WHEN TO SACK A PROFESSIONAL

Many individuals and companies do not have vast experience of dealing with professionals of one sort or another; for example, they may never have used a management consultant before. They may have had high expectations which are not being realised. How can they determine whether they would be better off with another firm or practice?

Talking to others with experience of the profession in question will assist in formulating an objective judgement as to whether the service which has been obtained is satisfactory. The initial expectations may have been wholly unrealistic — it might be pleasant to fantasise that the management consultant will overnight bring about a complete turnaround in the fortunes of the business in one particular area, but this would not be realistic.

However, most users of professional services will know when they are unhappy with the service and will be able to undertake some objective consideration as to whether or not they have been seriously let down. The following areas are worthy of examination.

Quality of service/results

Has the professional given good advice? Was it accurate or do you frequently find inaccuracies or examples where the professional has 'got it wrong'? Even where there have not been many such examples, has a fundamental mistake been made?

You are right to expect that the professional knows his area. If he does not then you will almost certainly be better off with another firm. Professionals are not infallible. Although there are usually built in mechanisms to help minimise errors — such as ensuring that junior members of professional firms are supervised by partners or other superiors, or there are consultation processes within the professional firm — mistakes can still be made.

If there has been an error which has caused you loss, then always consider demanding compensation. The professional will almost certainly be covered by professional indemnity insurance cover for such losses anyway. Do not shy away from bringing legal proceedings where necessary. How to go about this is addressed in Chapter 7.

There may be cases where no major mistake has been made, but the professional simply does not appear to be very knowledgeable about the areas on which you are consulting him. Warning signs in this area can be that he never seems to know the answer to any of the questions put to him over the telephone and always has to consult with colleagues or look the answer up subsequently. Alternatively, you may receive a letter which contradicts advice previously given, perhaps drafted in a rather oblique way. No professional likes to draw direct attention to mistakes made.

However, if you are in receipt of such a letter or other oral communication suggesting that a mistake has been made, then ask for an explanation and preferably put in writing your concern, so that it cannot be cast aside and not be properly addressed by the practice. The error may not matter and all professionals will make mistakes at one time or another. What you need to know is the significance of the mistake and what consequences will flow from that. The professional who fails to inform you that you will not be able to obtain planning permission for the office development which is the sole motive behind your proposed purchase of a patch of land, for example, has made a major error and you are right to expect compensation, if obtaining such permission was clearly within his professional remit.

Professionals may be reluctant to tell you about the mistake, and even if they inform you about it, they will feel a natural caution to spell out the dire consequences which flow from it, or it may not at that stage be clear what the consequences will be. Be persistent and demand to know. Until you know the effect of a mistake and its consequences, you will not be able properly to assess whether to continue to use that professional or not.

If the firm is open about a mistake, a compromise may be possible and the mistake constructively sorted out. Perhaps the firm will undertake the corrective work free of charge and not render a bill for the earlier work, or else offer you substantial compensation. If they keep as much as possible secret be concerned. Similarly, if they pick a scapegoat and sack an employee, ensure that you are happy that the individual was at fault. Be aware, however, that no firm is going to hand over evidence to enable you to sue them, so expect some reticence on the subject of mistakes. The best firms will be loyal to staff except in cases of severe wrongdoing. Such loyalty, when coupled with openness, makes for the best professional and client relationship.

It can be very difficult to judge the quality of advice obtained, aside from the issue of mistakes. A firm may advise on some of the major issues, but omit others or miss out some of the less significant areas, which are relevant, but not crucial. Without being an expert in the relevant area, it is impossible to know what is being omitted.

The way that companies often ascertain that the quality of the professional advice obtained is not as high as it might be can be by discussion with other companies involved in the same transaction or in the same area of business, or by consulting another professional firm in the same area for one particular matter. Often firms find that they cannot use their usual professional firm because for a particular task other companies already use the same firm and there is a conflict of interest which means that for this one transaction another firm must be used. This can result in a company, often for the first time, using another professional practice, and sometimes it can be an 'eye-opener'. Seeing how another firm operates gives a useful insight into how the first firm operates.

Reading relevant trade papers keeps companies abreast of developments in the area in which they are concerned, about which their professional advisers should be aware. If the professionals have to find out from you about changes in the law, for example, in an area relevant to your business, this suggests that they are not as up to date as they might be. This may cause you to begin to worry about the quality of the advice which they have been giving you.

Also, reading correspondence sent to your professional from professionals involved in the transaction acting for opposing parties, often your competitors, can help you to make a judgement about the quality of service with which you are being supplied. Ask your professional to give you copies of all letters he receives from the other side, even if you think they may be difficult to understand. Do not accept a refusal from your professional on the grounds that there is no need to bother you with this type of correspondence. This correspondence will assist in keeping you fully informed about the transaction or other matters, and you can obtain explanations from your professional adviser, if necessary.

Consult the employees within your company who deal with the professionals on a day-to-day basis as to what they think of the quality of advice received. A number of them may have had experience of using rival firms when they were employed with other companies and may be particularly well placed to undertake a comparison on quality of advice. You may employ the same type of professionals, your own employed accountants or barristers. They will assist in effecting a quality analysis.

There is no easy answer to assessing quality of advice, which is probably the most important factor when purchasing professional services. The hardest element to judge and the most important should not be ignored, but the problem of 'not knowing what you are missing' is a real one. Going to leading firms, the so-called 'flight to quality', may overcome some of the problems in ensuring quality, but even large, well-respected practices can make mistakes.

Keeping a look-out for evidence that mistakes have been made and reading carefully all advice given should ensure that you are better informed as to the accuracy of advice given and its comprehensiveness, so that you can then determine whether that standard is high enough or whether it has fallen to a level to make it sensible to sack the professional firm used.

One method of assessing quality not yet considered here is that of results. Do the solicitors win your cases? Do the management consultants improve the speed of your production line or ensure that you purchase an effective computer system? Is the building you have commissioned completed on time and within budget, and is it sufficiently aesthetically pleasing to the eye along with being a pleasant working environment? Does the company undertaking training of your employees succeed in ensuring that those employees become knowledgeable about the relevant area?

Always assess results and do not underestimate them. Most professionals will not guarantee results. If they are getting it wrong all the time, assess whether they are really the practice for you. If you seem to lose all your cases, did they advise you to settle early in what was a hopeless case? If the professional is a recruitment agency or headhunter, are all their appointees unsatisfactory? Have a regular, perhaps annual, procedure for assessing all professionals which you use and stick to it. Reach difficult decisions through consultation with colleagues on whether you wish to continue to employ each of your professional firms.

Consider employing several such firms in tandem, perhaps for certain discrete tasks, so that you can make comparisons with other firms. This can be a good way of easing in a new firm gradually, by giving them a small part of your work and building this up to a larger proportion if you are happy with them. This will keep all the firms employed 'on their toes' by introducing an element of competition and making them feel less secure as to the enduring nature of their retainer.

Quality is the most important and most nebulous and difficult element to judge. There are other factors which have been discussed elsewhere in this book which are easier to test in determining whether to sack a firm or not. These include the following criteria.

Speed

You will have your own expectations of how fast you expect your professional advisers to react to your requests for advice or assistance. If advice is not provided swiftly enough and you do not feel that the firm is prioritising your work sufficiently over their other clients, then consider sacking them. Before reaching a decision on this, first judge whether or not your expectations are realistic or not. Could any other firm achieve the results which you want in your time-scale? Perhaps you do not understand the nature of the task which the professional is doing on your behalf.

What is reasonable to expect will depend on the type of task given to the professional. Also, do not expect all jobs to be undertaken with the same level of urgency. Beware of describing all your work as urgent or you will simply not be believed eventually. All professionals have to balance the needs of all their clients and give attention to the most urgent job in hand. This can be one of the hardest aspects of being a successful professional. The talent of properly prioritising jobs is useful for all who operate in business.

However, if you inform your professional that a particular job is very urgent and that you must have the answer by a particular time, and he agrees and then does not produce the advice within your time-scale, consider whether you are using the right practice. For very important matters, being late once may be sufficient to make you feel so annoyed that you will immediately consider using another firm. Be conscious, though, that there will inevitably be some delay involved in choosing and appointing another practice and if you are in the middle of a very important deal and the deadline for one part has just been missed through your professional's tardiness, there may not be enough time to appoint someone else for this deal.

If deadlines are missed all the time consider consulting someone else within the practice. Keeping to deadlines is very much a personal characteristic and not necessarily indicative of an ethos within a firm. Use someone within the firm who is quicker. It may be preferable to use the top person's assistant who gets things done, rather than the expert himself who is always too busy to get your work done on time.

You will generally be aware if the speed of service is satisfactory and will then determine whether or not to go elsewhere. Unless there has been negligent delay (not unheard of), delay will simply be an annoyance and lead you to take work elsewhere rather than being an example of professional misconduct.

Practical advice

The question of whether a professional is able to communicate effectively with the client has been discussed earlier in this book (see pages 100–6). Is the advice you receive easy to understand and does it offer solutions or just raise seemingly insuperable problems? If you do not like the advice which you receive, this is not necessarily the fault of the professional. There may be no easy answer to your problem; there may be no legal way of achieving the result which you require.

If, on the other hand, you cannot understand what the professional is saying, then you probably have a genuine cause for complaint. Transferring to another practitioner within the same firm may solve the problem. If the firm is old-fashioned and uses archaic language or if they are too modern and write in jargon or 'computerspeak' which you cannot understand, this may run throughout the whole practice. It may be best to move to a firm able to communicate in simple English and explain problems clearly.

You may prefer a business adviser who gives solutions to problems rather than a professional who simply quotes from statutes or accounting standards. Alternatively, you may want to run your own business and only want a simple summary of the relevant law or standard, with no advice as to how you might put this into practice. What you choose will be your perogative, but both types of advice should be available. Exercise your choice.

As to the issue of sacking a professional, the practicality of the advice you are given will probably not change over time so this issue is likely to arise early in the relationship. This may lead to an early sacking of the professional. Where it is only a matter of weeks after a firm has begun acting for you, it is wise to give them the opportunity to change the way they advise you. Tell them your concerns and ask them to change the way they advise you, or suggest a change of personnel who are given the task of working for you, before going as far as sacking them. Alternatively, if they have operated for you in a particular way for years and appear 'stuck in their ways', they will find it difficult to change. However, new employees at the instructing company may be hired who have experience elsewhere and with other firms. Often they will reassess all professional firms who have been used and determine whether to continue to use them. This could result in a midstream sacking on the grounds of the extent to which the advice offered by the professional firm concerned is impractical.

Personality clashes

You may suddenly find that your work is being handled by an individual with whom you cannot work. Although efforts should be made by all parties to work together, there will be circumstances where individuals simply cannot get on. If the firm concerned cannot allocate you another professional within the firm with whom you can work instead, either because they refuse to accommodate your concern or because they are too small a practice to have more than one expert in one particular area, then you may determine no longer to use their services for that reason.

Fees

Considerable space has been allocated earlier in this book (see Chapter 4) to the question of professional fees. If fees are increased too much in any one period, then raise your concern. If no compromise can be agreed, then consider dispensing with the services of the firm, but first find out if any other firm can do your work for less. There is no point in appointing another firm in a fit of pique which charges more, or the same. You will inevitably incur costs in changing firms; the new firm will need to become acquainted with the work you require to be done and there will be an inevitable learning curve, usually at your expense.

Similarly, try to avoid appointing another firm which gives a very low quote, only to find that their quote was not the fully inclusive figure which you were using in your comparison with the charges of your existing firm, but was in fact a basic figure on top of which all sorts of extra charges are added, such as for each telephone call they make to you or each sheet of photocopying paper used in relation to your job. Get a comparable quote and agree a fixed period over which the rate is fixed. A low quote now in relation to charging rates, which are then subject to their annual, and usually upward, review in two months' time, may mean that the new firm is more expensive in the long run.

This is not to say that another firm will not be cheaper. They may well be, but ensure that they really are before moving to the new practice and dispensing with the services of the old.

SACKING AUDITORS

There are special rules concerning the sacking of auditors. Auditors are appointed by the company in general meeting, ie by the shareholders and are reappointed each year, usually at the annual general meeting of the company. They cannot be dismissed by the directors, only by the shareholders.

Where the auditors are removed by the shareholders of the company before the end of their appointed period of office, the Registrar of Companies must be informed within fourteen days of removal. Twenty-eight days' notice is required of a meeting to be held to dismiss an auditor before the expiry of his period of office. Auditors have the right to make representations in writing to the company. The company is required to forward these representations to the shareholders. If this is not done, the auditors have the right to be heard at the meeting.

SUMMARY OF STEPS IN DISMISSING A PROFESSIONAL ADVISER

The following is a summary of the steps you might take in dismissing a professional adviser:

1. Type of professional. If auditor, follow special rules (see above)

↓

2. Contract. Check the contract, if there is one, with the professional. Is there a fixed term? Are there rights to terminate on notice or for failure to perform adequately, or for any other reason?

↓

3. Is the professional in the middle of a job? Would it be better to leave him to complete the current work?

↓

4. Are you sure you wish to use another firm? It may simply be the individual you are using at the professional firm who is unsatisfactory. Consider asking for a change of personnel first.

↓

5. Have you complained? Depending on the nature of your complaint it may be easier to ask for an improvement first, rather than take the drastic step of moving to another firm.

↓
6. Inform the firm of your decision in writing. Do this by letter to the right person, only after you have found another firm willing to act, unless you want the first firm to have the opportunity to put their views first. Give reasons if you wish.
↓
7. Do not be persuaded against your will to remain with the firm. However, listen to their explanation.
↓
8. Prepare a list of outstanding matters and fees (if any). Ask for a similar list from the firm. Compare lists and sort out discrepancies.
↓
9. Arrange for the orderly transfer of files to your new adviser.

In this way a smooth transition to a new set of advisers can be achieved.

CHECKLIST

- Make complaints where justified, checking all the facts first and following any grievance procedure set out in your letter of appointment with the professional

- Where allegations of dishonesty are concerned, it may be imprudent to make a complaint to the dishonest adviser. Warn his professional body first

- When writing a letter dispensing with the services of a professional firm, ensure that the questions of outstanding fees and open files are addressed

- Judge whether to sack a professional or not by looking at not only the overall quality of service, but also the results generated by the firm, its speed in handling your matters, how practical and useful the advice from the adviser has been, whether you get on as people

- Follow the special rules in sacking auditors

7

Suing the professional

The profession, serving the vital needs of man, considers its first ethical imperative to be altruistic service to the client.

M L Cogan, 1953

In the previous chapter, consideration was given to sacking professional advisers and how to make complaints to professional bodies. First of all, in a situation where you are unhappy about the professional advice you have received and feel that the professional is at fault and, where appropriate, you have raised the matter with the firm concerned without receiving a satisfactory response, contact the relevant professional body, details of which appear in Appendix 2. There is no obligation to do so, however, and you can bypass this stage entirely and begin legal proceedings if you wish, or you may wish to follow both courses of action simultaneously.

COMPROMISE

**Always use legal proceedings as a last resort —
they are expensive.**

You may feel hurt and annoyed and think that you have been taken advantage of, but do you really want to pay another professional firm a lot more money in professional fees to make yourself feel better? You may end up feeling twice as bad. You may try and fail, and not only have to pay the solicitors who represented you in suing the firm of professional advisers, but also the costs of the firm which you have unsuccessfully tried to sue.

Think deeply before launching legal proceedings. Try to rise above your feelings. Many people hold very strong views about professionals, regarding them as playing on the misfortunes of others and making huge sums for doing virtually nothing, whilst others work very hard making goods to keep the country running. There are many misconceptions about professionals and their role. Many professionals do work extremely hard, some for modest sums, but their work is not on show. The hours spent on research are not apparent.

In practice, some of the complaints of users of professionals are justified and some of the prejudice against advisers is not. For the purposes of this chapter, the important thing is to divorce your feelings from your judgement when you contemplate suing professionals. If you find it difficult to do so, consider consulting a friend or colleague who is disinterested and can give you an unbiased view as to whether or not the professional really has done such a bad job that he should be sued.

Even where it appears objectively that there are grounds for proceedings to be brought, consider, as with any litigation, whether you can settle the matter amicably. Although it may go against the grain, it is wise to seek legal advice before settling, particularly if large sums are involved. It may not be sensible if future legal proceedings are considered to disclose to the professional firm all the details of your case in the hope of settling. However, if it is simply a matter of the firm having made a mistake, particularly when they have admitted it, and if the sum involved is fairly small, it may be possible to agree a figure as compensation without needing to instruct solicitors.

Whether solicitors are used or not, remember that it is much cheaper to settle than to litigate. Keep asking your solicitors how much the case has cost, and how much they expect it to cost throughout as the case develops, and always have one eye on whether the professional fees are beginning to get dangerously close to the sum you might recover if you sued, or even to exceed that sum.

If you are simply unhappy with a bill, you may be able to agree a reduction. This chapter is concerned with situations where you have suffered substantial losses through the actions of any sort of professional adviser.

---

1. Your IT management consultant arranges a computer system for you which is wholly inadequate. The system cannot do basic functions, which the adviser ought to have known were an integral part of your business.
2. Your accountant produces a so-called 'tax saving' scheme, which results in a large extra bill for the company from the Inland Revenue.
3. Your solicitor advises your company on the acquisition of a business, but fails to obtain adequate warranties from the purchaser. The business is worth nothing like the sum which you expected, but you have no legal recourse against the vendor.
4. Architects are responsible for a design error or have failed to take reasonable care in selecting contractors.
5. Surveyors perform a negligent survey.
6. Solicitors cause a plaintiff to lose the opportunity to bring an action or to acquire an interest in some property.
7. Accountants carry out a defective audit and a fresh audit has to be effected by another firm and paid for.

There are any number of other areas. The common thread is fault. When a compromise is not possible and you are unable to agree compensation with the adviser, even following a complaint to the professional body, you will need to consider taking legal proceedings against the firm.

COMPLAINTS TO PROFESSIONAL BODIES

Can the professional bodies be trusted to investigate? After all, they are mostly self-regulating, which means that the professions regulate themselves. In some cases, for example law, there is an ombudsman to whom a complaint can be made if you feel that you have not had your case adequately handled by the professional body. The Legal Services Ombudsman handles about 1200–1300 cases each year of which 90 per cent first went to the Solicitors Complaints Bureau. The Ombudsman has powers to consider compensation awarded by the Bureau and can recommend the payment of compensation, the highest in 1993 being in the region of £2000, although the Ombudsman has powers to order unlimited fines to be paid.

Would you be better off to sue straight away after efforts to settle with the firm have failed? There is no easy answer to this question. There is no general 'conspiracy' between professional bodies and their members. It is in the interests of professional bodies that they are seen to be thorough and scrupulous in their investigation of complaints. On balance you are likely to receive a fair hearing. However, do not regard a complaint to a professional body and legal proceedings as being mutually exclusive; the two often go in tandem.

Take the example of a fraudulent solicitor, who has made off with thousands of pounds of clients' money. On discovering the money was missing, you would complain to the professional body, inform the police and also sue for recovery of the money. Now, in such a case the individual may be bankrupt, but it is here that you are in a better position suing professionals, who are covered by 'indemnity' insurance, than suing other types of businesses. Most professionals will be insured against just such loss and the insurance will be compulsory. There will be a compensation fund to which recourse can be made if you are unable to recover your losses from the professional concerned.

Professional bodies can take years to investigate complaints. If you want compensation fairly quickly by all means complain to the professional body — it may result in the professional being struck off the register and thus rendered unable to cause similar losses to other companies — but consider suing too.

FINDING A LAWYER

Some solicitors specialise in cases involving actions against professionals. If you cannot find anyone prepared to take your case, the Law Society will undertake to find a solicitor for you. You do not need to use a solicitor to bring a court action. Those short of funds can take proceedings themselves, although the area of professional negligence is not straightforward in the way that recovering a debt owed is. A Law Centre or Citizen's Advice Bureau may be able to offer free advice.

Contract and tort

When you agree with your professional adviser that he will carry out work for you, you are entering into a contract with him, which contains an implied term that the work will be carried out with reasonable skill and care. The professions are different from other providers of goods or services in that success cannot always be guaranteed. Even when a solicitor has done the best he could in preparing a case for trial, the client may lose the action. This is not necessarily because of any fault on the part of the professional. There is, therefore, a difficult assessment to be made in each case of whether or not there has been a failure to meet the standard which it would be reasonable to expect of the relevant professional under consideration.

In addition to liability under contract, professionals may be 'negligent'. Negligence is a 'tort' or legal wrong. An action in negligence is possible whether or not there is a contract between the parties, provided the defendant owed a duty of care to the plaintiff and there has been a breach of that duty of care, as a consequence of which the defendant has suffered loss or damage.

Surveyors instructed by a building society to carry out a house valuation have been held to owe a duty of care to protect the mortgagor against losses flowing from a defective valuation. Auditors, in another case, were held not to owe a duty of care to individuals who might purchase shares in reliance on published accounts (in the House of Lords' *Caparo* decision).

The difficult question in each case will be whether or not the professional has met the standard of skill and care to be expected of an individual in that profession.

Immunity from suit and exclusion clauses

Barristers are immune from prosecution, but only in relation to work done in court. There are few professionals who are immune from legal actions. Some contracts with management consultants may contain clauses excluding liability, which are common in contracts for the supply of goods. Liability is often limited to replacing or repairing defective goods and all liability for financial and indirect loss is excluded. However, many professional bodies by regulation or the law forbid their members from excluding liability in this way.

For example, section 310 of the Companies Act 1985 forbids accountants to limit their liability by contract in this way. Some practices are considering ceasing to carry out auditing because of the increase in legal proceedings being taken against auditors. In 1993, the eight largest accountancy firms hired consultants to advise on a range of suggested reforms which might in the future (if adopted) include a limitation on the amount of damages which might be ordered against them.

The Solicitors Act 1974 s. 60(5) forbids solicitors excluding liability for contentious business (ie litigation — court actions).

Even where there are valid exclusion clauses, some statutes, such as the Unfair Contract Terms Act 1977 and the EC Directive on Unfair Contract Terms (when implemented in the UK), limit the extent to which such clauses will be enforceable if 'unreasonable' or 'unfair'.

PRACTICAL QUESTIONS

Whom to sue?

Most professionals work in partnerships. The partners are jointly and severally liable for the debts of the partnership without limit, even to the extent of their personal assets, except in so far as their homes and investments might be in the name of their spouse. Proceedings are brought against the partners of the firm. Some consultants and others operate through limited companies. For such companies legal proceedings should be brought against the company, in some cases joining individuals as parties to the action too.

What is recoverable?

When an action is successful, the plaintiff will recover damages, the aim of which is to put the plaintiff in the same position as if the negligence had never occurred. When an action is brought, the professional may counterclaim for recovery of his fees. These may or may not be payable, depending on the nature of the case and the quantity of work which has been undertaken.

When should proceedings be brought?

There is a period of six years dating from the time when a cause of action accrues in which to bring proceedings in relation to a 'tort' (ie breach of duty) or breach of contract action (under the Limitation Act 1980). Where damage is latent (ie concealed), there is an alternative period of three years in which to bring proceedings in negligence from the starting date as defined in the Act. The important point to note for those contemplating suing a professional adviser is that there is little merit in delay. Although the periods set out here appear to be lengthy, preparation of a case can take some time and the period may have already started to run. Proceed with reasonable speed to ensure that your claim is not time-barred.

CONCLUSION

In an ideal world it would never be necessary to bring legal proceedings against professional advisers. In practice, it may be necessary as a last resort. Due to the existence of compulsory indemnity insurance and compensation funds for some professions, those wronged by their professionals are in a stronger position than those suffering losses through the activities of general companies carrying on business, often with the protection which limited liability brings. However, never embark on legal action without considerable prior thought and advice and pursue all other avenues first.

CHECKLIST

- Only sue as a last resort
- Negotiate first
- Make a complaint to the relevant professional body or any relevant Ombudsman
- Use a solicitor familiar with the law of professional negligence
- Sue all the partners of a firm
- Ensure that proceedings are brought before the expiry of the relevant 'limitation period'

FIVE-POINT PLAN FOR A BETTER DEAL

Assuming that you already have a professional adviser, whom you wish to continue to instruct:

1. Obtain clarification in writing of the terms on which he is retained, unless this has already been done.
2. Hold a frank and open discussion of the costs, if this issue concerns you. Discuss:

   (a) estimates;
   (b) lower hourly charging rates, fixed for twelve/months, with annual review;
   (c) regular itemised bills;
   (d) a retainer or telephone 'hotline' service;
   (e) caps and fixed fees.

**Have in writing what you agree.
Keep a close watch on bills.**

---

3. Communicate regularly and clearly with your professional adviser. Keep him informed of developments in your business.
4. If you are unhappy, complain early. Do not let problems fester and grow.
5. Do not be fobbed off. If you are really concerned, change firms and/or complain of professional misconduct to the professional body and/or sue.

Appendix 1

SUMMARY OF CURRENT PROFESSIONAL ADVISERS AND THEIR FEES

Type of professional	Firm and contact name	Address and tel/fax	Bills — dates and amounts over last 12 months	Fee basis/ disputes
Accountants				
Solicitors				
Management Consultants				
Marketing and Advertising Advisers				
Surveyors				
Architects				
Patent/Trademark Agents				
Merchant Bankers				
Others				

Appendix 2

PROFESSIONAL BODIES

1. Accountants

The Institute of Chartered
Accountants of England and
Wales
PO Box 433
Chartered Accountants Hall
Moorgate Place
London EC2P 2BJ
Tel: 071–920 8100

The Institute of Chartered
Accountants of Scotland
27 Queen Street
Edinburgh EH2 1LA
Tel: 031–225 5673
Fax: 031–225 3813

The Chartered Institute of
Certified Accountants
29 Lincoln's Inn Fields
London WC2A 3EE
Tel: 071–242 6855
Fax: 071–831 8054

The Chartered Institute of
Management Accountants
63 Portland Place
London W1N 4AB
Tel: 071–637 2311

The Chartered Institute
of Public Finance and
Accountancy
3 Robert Street
London WC2N 6BH
Tel: 071–930 3456

2. Solicitors

The Law Society
113 Chancery Lane
London WC2A 1PL
Tel: 071–242 1222
Fax: 071–405 9522

Complaints addressed to the:
Solicitors Complaints Bureau
Victoria House
8 Dormer Place
Royal Leamington Spa
Warwickshire CV32 5AE.

Legal executives:
The Institute of Legal
Executives
Kempston Manor
Kempston
Bedford MK42 7AB
Tel: 0234 841000

3. Barristers

The General Council of the Bar
3 Bedford Row
London WC1R 4DB
Tel: 071–242 0082
Fax: 071–831 9217

4. Management Consultants

The Institute of Management
  Consultants
5th Floor
32/33 Hatton Garden
London EC1N 8DL
Tel: 071–242 2140
Fax: 071–831 4597

Management Consultancies
  Association
11 West Halkin Street
London SW1X 8JL
Tel: 071–235 3897
Fax: 071–235 0825

The Institute of Personnel
  Management
IPM House
35 Camp Road
London SW19 4UX
Tel: 081–946 9100
Fax: 081–947 2570

Institute of Training and
  Development
Marlow House
Institute Road
Marlow
Bucks SL7 1BD
Tel: 0628 890123
Fax: 0628 890208.

Computing Services Association
Hanover House

73–74 High Holborn
London WC1V 6LE
Tel: 071–405 2171

The Chartered Institute of
  Building
Englemere
Kings Ride
Ascot
Berkshire SL5 8BL
Tel: 0344 874545
Fax: 0344 23467

5. Marketing and Advertising Advisers

The Advertising Association
Abford House
15 Wilton Road
London SW1V 1NJ
Tel: 071–828 2771
Fax: 071–931 0376

The Direct Marketing
  Association
1 Haymarket House
London SW1Y 4EE
Tel: 071–321 2525
Fax: 071–321 0191

The Chartered Institute of
  Marketing
Moor Hall
Cookham
Maidenhead
Berkshire SL6 9QH
Tel: 0628 524922
Fax: 0628 531382

Institute of Public Relations
The Old Trading House
15 Northburgh Street
London EC1V 0PR

Tel: 071–253 5151
Fax: 071–490 0588

Public Relations Consultants
  Association
Willow House
Wilton Place Victoria
London SW1P 1JH
Tel: 071–233 6026
Fax: 071–828 4797

6. Surveyors

The Royal Institution of
  Chartered Surveyors
12 Great George Street
Parliament Square
London SW1V 3AD
Tel; 071–222 7000
Fax: 071–222 9430

Publications address:
Surveyor Court
Westwood Business Park
Westwood Way
Coventry CV4 8JE

7. Architects

The Architects Registration
  Council of the United
  Kingdom (ARCUK)
73 Hallam Street

London W1N 6EE
Tel: 071–580 5861
Fax: 071–436 5269

Many architects are members of:
The Royal Institute of British
  Architects
66 Portland Place
London W1N 4AD
Tel: 071–580 5533
Fax: 071–255 1541

8. Patent and Trademark Agents

The Chartered Institute of Patent
  Agents
Staple Inn Buildings
High Holborn
London WC1V 7PZ
Tel: 071–405 9450
Fax: 071–430 0471

The Institute of Trade Mark
  Agents
4th Floor
Canterbury House
2–6 Sydenham Road
Croydon CRO 9XE
Tel: 081–686 2052
Fax: 081–680 5723

Appendix 3

LETTER CLARIFYING TERMS

[On your notepaper]

[Date   19   ]

[Firm's address and
reference
              ]

Dear Mr [   ],

[XYZ & Co Ltd]

Further to our meeting on [19   ], I am writing to confirm
that we wish to instruct your firm to advise us in connection
with [   ].

1. We agreed that your assistant [Mr/s   ] would [ADD
FULL DETAILS OF THE WORK TO BE DONE] by [19   ]. I am
available all week if [he] requires further information.

2. You informed me that your hourly charging rate is normally
[£   ] and your assistant's [£   ], but that you would
discount your rates by 10% for our work and freeze them at their

current level for twelve months from the date of our meeting. I hope we can meet in twelve months' time to discuss rates for next year.

3. You estimated that the cost of doing this work would be [£   ]. We agreed that you would let me know when your fees approached this figure, before further work was undertaken.

4. You informed me that you will send us bills monthly and require payment within thirty days of invoice. We agreed that bills would clearly show (i) the work done, (ii) the individual undertaking the work and (iii) the cost of their time and the discount applied. We appreciate your accommodating our need for itemised billing. The provision of esitmates gives us greater certainty and allows us properly to budget for professional fees.

I look forward to hearing from you.

Yours sincerely,
[Signature]

Appendix 4

SPECIMEN LETTER OF COMPLAINT

[On your notepaper]

[Date   19]

[Firm's address and
reference
               ]

Dear Mr [   ],

Work undertaken for XYZ & Co Ltd

We have spoken informally on a number of occasions over the last few
months, including last on [19   ] on the subject of your firm's
services to this company.

As matters do not appear to have improved I wish to confirm in writing
our concerns.
[SET THEM OUT, BEING AS SPECIFIC AS POSSIBLE, SUCH AS —
WE SENT YOU A LETTER ON 28TH MARCH AND YOU REPLIED
TWO WEEKS LATER DESPITE OUR LETTER STRESSING TO YOU
THE URGENCY AND OUR SUBSEQUENT TELEPHONE CALL TO
YOU. COMPLAINTS MAY INCLUDE:

- work produced slowly;
- work rushed and inaccurate;
- instructions not followed;
- bills too high or non-specific;
- different employees/partners each time;
- too many people working on one job;
  etc, etc]

I hope that we can agree how we can proceed for the future to improve the position. Perhaps a meeting to discuss the issue raised in this letter would assist. Provided this problem can be settled to our satisfaction, we hope to continue to instruct you in the future.

I look forward to hearing from you.

Yours sincerely,
[Signature]

[CONSIDER COPYING TO THE PARTNER CONCERNED OR THE SENIOR PARTNER, IF YOU HAVE COMPLAINED VERBALLY BEFORE TO NO EFFECT]

SPECIMEN LETTER TERMINATING YOUR RELATIONSHIP WITH YOUR PROFESSIONAL ADVISER

[On your notepaper]

[Date   19]

[Firm's address and
reference
            ]

Dear Mr [   ],

XYZ & Co Ltd

I am writing formally to inform you that we have appointed another firm to undertake our work in the [   ] area.

I enclose our statement of your outstanding bills. Please prepare a statement and bills on all outstanding matters to the date of this letter as soon as possible, in particular summarising what stage our various [files] have reached.

To ensure a smooth handover, please send your files [to me for forwarding to our new advisers — IF YOU DO NOT WANT TO NAME THE NEW FIRM] *or* [to ABC & Co.] as soon as possible.
Or [As the [   ] matter is so far advanced, we would like you to continue to handle that until completion, so please proceed as usual in relation to that matter.]

I look forward to hearing from you.

Yours sincerely,
[Signature]

[IF YOU BELIEVE THAT YOU HAVE ANY GROUNDS TO SUE THE FIRM OR HAVE ANY SORT OF LEGAL DISPUTE WITH THEM, THEN DO NOT SEND ANY LETTER WITHOUT SEEKING PRIOR LEGAL ADVICE, IN ORDER TO ENSURE THAT YOU DO NOT PREJUDICE YOUR POSITION IN ANY LETTER.]

Appendix 5

GUIDE BOOKS LISTING PROFESSIONAL SERVICES

Companies and professional bodies produce lists of their members, which are obtainable from public libraries and bookshops. These will not always list the professionals according to specialisation. A selection is listed below.

1. The *Legal 500* by John Pritchard, which is published annually by Legalease, 28–33 Cato Street, London W1H 5HS, Tel: 071–396 9292, Fax: 071–396 9300/9301. This contains full details of specialisations, including commentary on the recognised best practices for different types of work.
2. *Chambers and Partners' Directory*, edited by Michael Chambers, Chambers and Partners Publishing, 74 Long Lane, London EC1A 9ET, Tel: 071–606 2266. Published annually, this contains full details of specialisations and commentary on the practices and names individual experts.
3. *The Commercial Bar Directory*, Chancery Law Publishing, 22 East-castle Street, London W1N 7PA. This gives specialisations of barristers' chambers.
4. *The Law Society's Directory of Solicitors and Barristers*, obtainable from the Law Society (see Appendix 2).
5. *Butterworths Law Directory*, Reed Information Services Limited, Windsor Court, East Grinstead House, East Grinstead, West Sussex RH19 1XA, Tel: 0342 335890, Fax: 0342 317422.
6. *The Bar Directory*, the General Council of the Bar/Legalease Limited, 28–33 Cato Street, London W1H 5HS, Tel: 071–396 9292, Fax: 071–396 9300/9301. This lists barristers.

7. *The Institute of Chartered Accountants in England and Wales Directory of Firms*, available from the ICA, details in Appendix 2. Lists members of the ICA both geographically and alphabetically.
8. *Management Consultants in the UK*, TFPL Publishing, 76 Park Road, London NW1 4SH, Tel: 071–251 5522, Fax: 071–251 8318.
9. *Chartered Patent Agents*, Charles Letts & Co Ltd/Chartered Institute of Patent Agents, Letts of London House, Parkgate Road, London SW11 4NQ, Tel: 071–407 8891, Fax: 071–407 5357. This describes the profession, and also lists agents at the back.
10. *Chartered Institute of Patent Agents' Membership List*, published annually, obtainable from the Chartered Institute of Patent Agents, Staple Inn Buildings, High Holborn, London WC1V 7PZ, Tel: 071–405 9450, Fax: 071–430 0471.

Those publications which categorise the professionals according to their specialisations and name the reputed experts in each field are a particularly useful aid in choosing a firm.

Index